ATTRACTING

NEW

MEMBERS

ATTRACTING

NEW

MEMBERS

by

Robert L. Bast

co-published by

REFORMED CHURCH IN AMERICA
New York, NY

&

CHURCH GROWTH, INC.
Monrovia, CA

Library of Congress Catalog Card No. 82-69771
ISBN 0-932208-13X

Printed in U.S.A.

A Word of Thanks

With the advances of research and study of congregational outreach in the past two decades, the issues discussed in this book have been dealt with by numerous authorities, whose knowledge and skill have enriched all of us. I am personally indebted to many people from whom I have learned. The sources which are referred to on the following pages have been my teachers and companions. Others, whose ideas have influenced my thinking, go unmentioned, simply because I have absorbed their material and forgotten the source. It is important for me to say, in a paraphrase of St. Paul, that I have nothing which I did not receive.

The work of Lyle Schaller, Ben Johnson, Herb Miller, and The Alban Institute have been particularly important sources for me, and I am most grateful for what I have learned from them. However, I owe the greatest debt to Church Growth, Inc., and in particular to Win Arn, Bob Orr, and Charles Arn. From the beginning of my service as the Reformed Church in America's Minister for Evangelism, they have showed unfailing kindness and helpfulness. They have shared their knowledge, materials, and even their building. They have met with our denomination's evangelism team and evaluated our plans for evangelism. They have, most generously, offered their considerable skills and knowledge to us, and we are deeply in their debt. A further evidence of their graciousness is the invitation extended to me to write this volume. They have been my teachers, mentors, colleagues, and friends, and I am most thankful for them.

On a personal level, I wish to recognize and thank the many friends, colleagues, and family, whose love supports and enriches me, and whose prayers have sustained me. In particular, I thank my wife Jan, for her unfailing love and patience, as well as her valuable comments on the manuscript, and our daughter, Cathleen Bast Holbrook, for her most helpful work in editorial improvement. Thanks also, to my secretary, Ines Madderom, for coping graciously and efficiently with extra responsibilities, and typing the manuscript through several revisions. My love and gratitude is also expressed to the congregation of Garfield Park Reformed Church in Grand Rapids, Michigan. In a joy-filled thirteen-year ministry together, we learned much of what now finds its way into this book. To my friends there, shalom.

This book is dedicated with love and gratitude to those who have served on the Evangelism Development Team of the Reformed Church in America:

> Joyce de Velder
> Dave Dethmers
> Ken Eriks
> Mary Fitzgerald
> Don Jansma
> Fritz Kruithof
> Michael Otte
> Gene Pearson
> Andy Rienstra
> Carl Vogelaar

CONTENTS

Introduction

At least three different types of evangelism can be found in the New Testament. There is the evangelism of personal witness, as demonstrated, for example, by Andrew. After meeting Jesus, Andrew "first found his brother Simon, and said to him, 'We have found the Messiah.' He brought him to Jesus" (John 1:41, 42). Does "first" mean finding Simon was the first thing Andrew did, as the New International Version assumes, or was Simon the first of many Andrew sought out and brought to Jesus? In either case Andrew's act is impressive. Andrew is, of course, only one example of this kind of evangelism.

A second type of New Testament evangelism is that of public proclamation. The book of Acts has many examples, of which Peter's sermon on the day of Pentecost is one outstanding illustration. So powerful was the message that people interrupted Peter before he had finished to ask, "What shall we do?" (See Acts 2:36-41). The conversion of 3,000 people is an indication of the power and effectiveness of proclamation evangelism.

A third type of evangelism can also be discovered in Acts 2. We may call this type evangelism through the attracting power of the Christian community. Acts 2:41-47 describes the early church in terms of what it was and what it did. As it lived out its transformed life, it made an impact on the people who came to know it, and drew many of them into its fellowship. As a result, "the Lord added to their number day by day those who were being saved" (Acts 2:47).

Most of the people who make up the membership of the Christian church today have been brought to faith by this third method of evangelism. As the Christian church, gathered in congregations like yours, lives out its life and carries out its mission, it attracts people who come to know it, and God brings them to faith.

All three types of evangelism are valid and necessary today. God's people hope and pray for the effectiveness of each method. A further hope is for an increasing demonstration of the effective integration of the three methods. This happens when 1) the members of Christian churches share their faith and bring their friends and relatives to their congregations, 2) where the good news is proclaimed and 3) the life of the congregation draws people in and calls forth faith.

This is a book about one key part in that process. It explores ways in which churches can attract new members and bring them into the family.

Preparing to Attract Visitors

As a rule, a typical congregation will lose about six percent of its members each year. Some will move away and join other churches. Some will die, and some will drop out. Large churches, and those in transitional areas, will lose a higher percentage—perhaps 10% of their members. If we think of a typical congregation of 200 members, we may expect that they will lose about 12 members each year.

In order to grow, that church will first need to replace the members who have been lost. In the case of our example, the congregation will need to bring 13 people into its fellowship before it begins to experience any growth.

A False Assumption About How Churches Grow

Where do new members come from? An assumption which has been made by many people is that growth happens naturally. The idea is that the church will grow as the children of the members grow up and take their place in the congregation, and as new people seek out the church and affiliate with it.

Is this assumption correct? Usually not. It is hard to imagine that any church will grow by relying on these two factors. Very few congregations will be successful in simply replacing membership losses through these means. Let's take a moment to look at each assumption.

Children of members are a very unlikely source of future membership. You might try this experiment. Calculate the total number of children in your congregation who have not yet become active members. What will happen if all those children eventually join your church? Will you have 6% increases each year, as we have suggested are needed if you are to simply maintain present membership levels? Generally speaking, even if all the children who are part of the church remain there as adult members, your congregation will not grow.

There are two reasons why children of members are unlikely to bring about growth in the congregation. For one thing, as a rule we have smaller families than previous generations, so there are fewer children among our church families. More significantly, most of the children who grow up in our congregations will not be there as adult members. They move away or drift away or join another congregation. While I do not know of any studies which have been done on this subject, I would guess that in many congregations fewer than ten percent of the children who have grown up in the church will be found in that congregation as adult members.

The assumption that people will seek out the church on their own is also highly questionable.

They are not likely to seek out a church because of its denominational identity, since denominational loyalty can no longer be anticipated. People join congregations, not denominations, and so they will not show up because of a sign on the church property. Nor are they likely to appear on their own. Research has been developed on the subject of what brought first-time visitors to church. This study was conducted by Church Growth, Inc.,[1] and the results have been confirmed by other studies, including a recent one by The Alban Institute.[2] The conclusion was that only about nine percent of all adults who join a church seek it out on their own. We certainly cannot rely on waiting for people to come to us if we intend to grow.

True Assumptions

Let's look at two more helpful assumptions:

#1 *Churches that grow are intentional about it; they plan to grow.*

#2 *Churches that grow are working at it; they do things which facilitate growth.*

Intentional and active ... these are two of the keys to growth.

A church committed to growth will have spent time on the question we posed earlier: "Where are our new members to come from?" They may have come up with several answers, and set in place plans and programs to reach people in a variety of ways. One answer they will have identified is: "from visitors who attend our worship services."

The visitors we plan to reach are those who live within the ministry area of our church, and are not currently involved in the life of any worshipping congregation. When using the term "visitor" in this book, we are restricting its meaning to this specialized sense. How many visitors do we hope to attract? Rather than simply saying "as many as we can", let's think about the question. Suppose our hypothetical congregation of 200 members has set a goal of adding 25 new members to the church this year. Typically, about 15 percent of first time worship visitors ultimately join the congregation they initially visit. These are the people you hear say: "This was the first congregation I attended when I decided to go back to church. I liked it so well I never went anywhere else." If we choose to operate on the basis of statistical probability, we can say that if we attract 167 first-time visitors, we will be likely to gain 25 new members. We need to recognize, of course, that this means 167 different people, or an average of more than three first-time visitors each Sunday.

If the first-time visitor returns for a second visit within a few weeks, the probability of that person joining the congregation increases dramatically. About two-thirds of the people who visit a church twice within a brief time period are likely to join that congregation. In terms of probability, again, we may conclude that if we can attract 38 second-time visitors we will probably reach our goal of 25 additions.

Some fascinating recent research clarifies the picture even more. Twenty congregations were surveyed on the question of what percentage of their first-time visitors returned for a second visit. Responses ranged from a low of five percent to a high of 40 percent. In other words, congregations that did nothing to respond to the needs and opportunities of visitors still found that about five

percent of their first-time visitors made their way
back.   On the other hand, congregations doing
absolutely the best job in ministering to visitors
found that in spite of their efforts, less than half
their first-time visitors returned.

Adding this data to the mix, we may say that
a 25 percent rate of visitor return is near the
average. To continue our statistical analysis, we
can carry our projection one step further. If we are
doing a fairly good job in our ministry with visitors,
and are at least average in communicating a
positive response, about 25 percent of our first-time
visitors will return. We have said we need about 38,
so we can now determine that we need to attract
about 150 first-time visitors to reach our goal of 25
new members.

It has now become clear that two questions
need to be addressed: how do we attract first-time
visitors? and, how do we attract them to return?
Those are two of the questions this book will attempt
to answer.

Attracting Visitors — Where Do They Come From?

What do you think of when you hear the
word "attract"? Several different meanings may
come to mind, and looking at a few will be a good
way to begin to understand our task. To "attract"
means:

- to get someone's attention, as when we wave
  to the person for whom we are saving a seat;
- to draw toward, as when using a magnet;
- to feel affection for, as in friendship or
  romance; and
- to awaken interest, as in "previews of coming
  attractions."

So then, the image of attraction suggests that the church needs to get people's attention and awaken their interest in such a way as to draw them to the church and enable them to feel the love of the people in the church and the Lord of the church. That requires the development of plans and methods. A crucial principle to remember is this: the essence of attracting lies in having something worthwhile to offer.

In developing a strategy for attracting visitors, many congregations have found it helpful to begin by appointing a church growth task force. This will usually be a group of five to seven people who have been selected to help the congregation plan its outreach ministry. They will be representative of different groups in the congregation, will include both recent and long-time members, and be positive people who are enthused about the church and its present ministry. They will focus their efforts in several key areas.

Understanding Your Community

Not all congregations have the same potential in attracting worship visitors. One of the most important factors is one over which we have little control, and that is the demographic data about the number and kinds of people who live in the church neighborhood. Some churches have far greater prospects than others. While circumstances vary widely, virtually every congregation has reachable unchurched people living around it.

A community survey can help you better understand and identify the persons in your community who are prospective visitors to your church. The purpose of a community survey is to learn about those people. It may be helpful if the task force seeks to discover answers to the following questions:

1. *What is our ministry area?*

We may assume that people will generally be willing to drive up to 20 minutes to attend church. One way to answer this question is simply to drive 20 minutes in each direction from your church building, note where you are, and draw a circle which connects each of the points to which you drove. Everything within the circle is thus in your ministry area. It is helpful, however, to go beyond that. Where do your present members live? Since present members are an important resource in reaching out to unchurched people, it will be wise to focus on the areas where many of your present members live. How large an area can you effectively address? You may want to concentrate your primary effort on a particular section.

2. *What is our target group?*

An advertisement in a recent issue of AMERICAN DEMOGRAPHICS magazine caught my eye. Addressed to people with something to sell, the text pointed out that there is no such thing as an "average person," and the only way to be effective in "selling" is to know whom you are trying to reach and gear your message to that group. A target audience allows for a program to reach specific people. These are people who have something in common, and who can be found in your ministry area in sufficient numbers that a ministry effort to reach them is desirable.

Who are the people in your ministry area that you have the best potential to reach? There will be many different groups of people in your community and one congregation cannot reach all groups. It is best to focus on specific groups which you have the potential to reach. This may require some survey work to learn about the make-up of the people in your community. Are there a significant number of single parent families? Young, two-career couples? Older adults? What resources do you have for ministry to one or more of these groups? The key resource needed is church members who are in the same category. They are needed to reach out to the target group and to welcome and help incorporate those who respond.

Do you see the possibility of identifying a particular group as one on which you will focus a ministry effort? This does not mean neglecting other people. It simply means that in addition to a general effort to reach all, your congregation has a specific approach to reaching some.

3. *What unmet needs can we identify in this target group which our congregation can address?*

A ministry which responds to the needs of people is an end, not a means to an end. Jesus healed sick people because they were sick, not in order to get them to follow him. Churches that minister in Jesus' name endeavor to help heal the hurts of humankind. That is what churches are intended to do.

This issue is raised here, however, in the recognition that people are often brought to faith as a result of a need being met. One thinks, for example, of the account of Jesus and the hemorrhaging woman (Mark 5:21-24) whose physical healing led to her salvation. Similarly, as the church addresses human needs, bridges are built on which we meet people who may be brought to faith. The meeting of their need becomes an opportunity to invite their participation in the life of the church.

Some congregations have found it helpful to do a "needs assessment" survey in their ministry area. A good way to do this is to have the task force go out on a Saturday morning and talk with about 100 people selected at random. Many people will be met outdoors (if the weather is appropriate) and can be interviewed on the spot. Richard Warren, a California pastor whose church has a remarkable ministry of outreach, used the following questions:

- What is the greatest need in this area?
- Why do you think most people do not attend church?
- Suppose you were looking for a church, what would you look for?
- What advice would you give to a church that wants to help people?[3]

The answers to these and similar questions may be tabulated and provide important information on needs and opportunities to which the congregation can respond.

The Importance of Community Ministry

When a congregation addresses itself to needs in its community, results often go beyond what is expected. In a congregation in Grand Rapids, Michigan, a young adult class took on as a project the painting of houses for those who could not afford to pay for it. In the first painting project, a young man from the community rode by on his bike and stopped to find out what was going on. He was so impressed that he showed up for worship the next day, and eventually became an active Christian and an effective leader in that congregation. Some other things were going on in this man's life which contributed to his decision, but the point is that the ministry addressed to meeting needs was the precipitating factor in his decision to become involved in the life of that congregation.

A few years ago the Presbyterian Church published a small book called *Vital Signs*.[4] In it they reported on ten of their congregations that were effective in ministry and experiencing growth. These congregations were deliberately selected to be as different as possible. The challenge was then to see what they had in common. After all the variables had been removed, only two factors could be identified which all the churches had in common: vital worship, and a ministry which addressed needs in the community.

Before leaving the subject of the community, it might be well to reflect on the number of unchurched people who live around us. More than three-fourths of the people in the United States now live in metropolitan areas. A typical suburban metropolitan church has 75,000 people in its ministry area. The latest Gallup poll survey indicates that 44% of the people in the United States have no involvement in any religious institution.[5] That could mean you have 30,000 or more unchurched people in your ministry area. The Gallup Poll, in its annual survey of unchurched Americans, asks whether the unchurched person is now, or might be in the future, open to participating in a religious community. According to Gallup, 58 percent of the unchurched responded positively to that question.[6] Just imagine, there may be more than 15,000 people living near your church who are reachable. Another way of looking at this is to assume that about 20 percent of the people in your ministry area are reachable, unchurched people. Which of them are being evangelized by your congregation?

You have just asked one of the most important questions your congregation needs to consider. It is a question which cannot be dealt with casually or quickly. If your congregation is to adequately deal with this question, at least two things need to happen:

1. The setting forth of a vision of the congregation as an evangelizing community.

A congregation needs to be challenged to recognize the crucial necessity of evangelism. One of the great responsibilities of the leaders of the church is to set a vision before the congregation of what God is calling it to be. In the pastor's leadership role, perhaps no task is more important than that of being a visionary leader. Through preaching, teaching, writing and conversation, the pastor continually sets this vision before the congregation, so that they recognize the challenge of evangelism and each person's responsibility to participate in the ministry of outreach.

One congregation I know of prints a one-sentence question in each Sunday's bulletin. The question is: "Who will you seek to evangelize this week?" That is just one illustration of how the challenge of being an evangelizing people can be set before the congregation. And it must be done regularly and creatively.

2. The second task which needs to accompany the raising of the evangelizing question is the ministry of prayer.

Each week prayers from the pulpit should include the mission of the congregation, the task of evangelization and the challenge for all members to participate. Prayer groups in the congregation should regularly include prayer for the ministry of the church. Each member of the congregation should be encouraged to pray regularly for those who have not yet come to believe, and for the church's efforts to reach them. Prayer is crucial to the evangelizing effort of the congregation.

We have begun to lift up a way by which a congregation can begin to focus its outreach effort. We are now ready to turn to a new question in our study.

---

1 Win Arn and Charles Arn, *The Master's Plan,* Pasadena, Church Growth Press, 1982, p. 43.
2 Roy Oswald and Speed Leas, *The Inviting Church,* Washington, The Alban Institute, 1987, pp 28, 39.
3 Quoted in *FOCUS,* Concepts of Ministry and Goals for the Local Church (Christian Reformed Home Missions, 1987), p. 38.
4 Wesley Baker, *The Vital Signs,* A Good News Evangelism Booklet. (New York: The Program Agency, The United Presbyterian Church in the USA, 1978).
5 Gallup, George, *The Unchurched American, 1988,* (Princeton: The Gallup Organization), pp. 4, 66.
6 Gallup, p. 102.

Reflection Questions — Chapter One

1. The introduction suggests three types of evangelism are to be found in the New Testament.
   - Do you believe all are valid and necessary today?
   - Which method do you believe you can be involved in?
   - Which method needs most emphasis in your church just now?
2. Chapter One makes the point that the growth of the church is not something that just happens naturally.
   - Do you agree or disagree?   Why?
3. "Churches that grow are intentional about it; they plan to grow. Churches that grow are doing things that facilitate growth." How true are these statements for your congregation?
4. What strategy for attracting visitors to your church do you think would be appropriate and effective?
5. What groups of people do you think your congregation has the best potential for reaching?
6. What community ministry does your congregation currently carry out?
   Can you think of an appropriate ministry you could begin?
7. On a scale of 1-10, what mark would you give your congregation for its commitment to be an evangelizing congregation?
8. What place does evangelization have in the prayers offered in your church? In your prayers?

Attracting and Keeping Visitors

In their book, *The Inviting Church,*[1] Roy Oswald and Speed Leas indicate that churches which do well in attracting new people generally have certain things in common which include:

1.   A Positive Identity and Self Image

Two issues are included in this concern. Congregations equipped for growth have a positive self-image.   That is, the members have good feelings about their congregation.   Congregations equipped for growth also have a positive identity. That is, the members believe their congregation is special and they have something unique to offer. These characteristics underlie and motivate the outreach ministry of the congregation.   They have to do with the desire and ability to reach out.

2.   Congregational Harmony

Congregations equipped for growth are unified congregations. There are no major conflicts within the church, and there is an essential agreement about the style and ministry of the congregation. The people of the congregation love and care for one another. Unity is a key to growth.

3.   Pastoral Enthusiasm

Congregations equipped for growth have enthusiastic pastors. Pastors who affirm, as well as challenge, the congregation. Pastors who are enthused with the potential of the church. Pastors full of hope who inspire joy and confidence in the members of the congregation. Pastors whose worship leadership is energetic and enthusiastic.

4.   Ministry in the Community

Congregations equipped for growth nearly always have some specific ministry in the community.   This community ministry authenticates and affirms the church's message of love. The ministry in the community helps people believe the word proclaimed and makes invitations from the congregation more readily accepted.

5.   Small Group Opportunities

Congregations equipped for growth have various small group opportunities which serve as entry points for new members. These small groups provide for people to become friends, and to deepen relationships. They represent a variety of interests and activities to which people can be invited and where they can become known.

Church Growth Task Force Responsibilities

A congregation does well to appoint a special growth task force to examine these five "common denominators" of attractive churches in relation to their own situation. In addition, your task force would have other tasks to carry out:

1. Review Your Church's Mission Statement

Does your church have a mission or purpose statement? A mission statement is a brief one or two sentence expression of your congregation's commitment to ministry. The purpose of such a statement is to clarify your aim and unify your congregation in support of your church's ministry. Here is an example of one congregation's ministry or mission statement:

> "We are people committed to the glory of God, providing worship, fellowship, member care, education, evangelism, and social action so that many people become disciples of Jesus Christ, incorporated into the nurturing and serving fellowship of the church living obediently before him in the world. (I Corinthians 10:30 and Matthew 28:19-20) [2]

Is your mission or purpose statement known and accepted? Is it still fresh and accurate? Does it guide you and keep you focused on outreach? Is it a reflection of the congregation's identity and intention? Are the groups and organizations in the congregation committed to implement it? Would reviewing or rewriting it help unify the congregation in a commitment to outreach?

2. Study Your Congregation's Membership

To begin, review your congregation's membership statistics for the past five years. For each year calculate the number of new members received, listing those who came by transfer from another church, those who came as a result of a spiritual awakening or conversion, and those who joined from among the children of the church. Total the result for each year. Then calculate members lost each year by death, transfer out, or dropping out. When you have the total, calculate the percentage of adult members gained for the year, and the percentage of adult members lost. In a healthy church, the percentage of gain will probably be four or more points higher than the percentage of loss.

The next step is to discover the age-range of your membership. List the number of members you have in each of the following age groups: 18-25; 26-40; 41-55; 56-65; 65 + over.

What is the purpose of this activity? It has a dual purpose: to add to your understanding of the present make-up and relative strengths of your church, and to plan your ministry effort.

We will take time to look at each of these groups, not primarily to think of life-issues with which they are dealing (although that does become important when exploring ministry efforts to reach one of these groups) but to look at some general patterns of interest and involvement in the church for each of these age groups. Remember that we are suggesting general characterizations, and there will be many exceptions. A word or phrase summarizes the key factor.

Age 18-25 "Inactivity"

As a rule, 18-25 year olds are not involved in the church in high numbers. Many people in this age group "drop-out" for a time — often seven to eight years. Research by The Alban Institute demonstrated that during the drop-out period most of these people do not stop believing and are not hostile to the church. They do tend to make their way back into the church, usually at about the age of 25 or 26. [3]

Age 26-40 "Opportunity"

The fastest growing group in American society, this is the baby-boom generation. It is the most reachable segment of the adult population. One key reason is that the arrival and the needs of children are one of the prime factors in bringing unchurched persons into the church. Family issues are a vital bridge to ministry with this group.

A significant amount of research has been done on this segment of the population, and evangelism conferences have been planned around the theme "Reaching the Baby-Boom Generation." Research is available which highlights the characteristics of this age group and suggests issues to be kept in mind in planning ministry with them.

It is widely accepted that people in this age group have a broad range of interests and concerns, and a wide variety of program options can be planned as part of a ministry to reach them. The baby-boom generation has within it many people who are looking for:
  • a spiritual experience which brings them closer to God;
  • Biblical knowledge which relates to life;

- an opportunity to discuss life's concerns and faith questions;
- help with family issues;
- a sense of belonging;
- an opportunity to serve in an important cause;
- the development of deeper interpersonal relationships;
- a chance for leadership.

Any congregation serious about growth will have a plan for reaching out to this age group.

Churches that have demonstrated effectiveness in reaching the baby-boom generation usually share a combination of common characteristics, which include:

- a strong worship focus;
- a meaningful educational program for all ages;
- an orientation toward experience and practical action, rather than a focus on intellectual and theoretical approaches;
- a high degree of tolerance and an acceptance of diversity;
- an emphasis on inclusion, with a particular concern to include women and newcomers in leadership;
- an informal style which is highly relational.

Another reason for describing the 26-40 year olds as the age of opportunity is that in most congregations, this will be the group that provides the largest number of the volunteer workers in the congregation, particularly in the areas of outreach and nurture.

Age 41-55 "Leadership" -

In most congregations, the leaders come from this group. Interesting dynamics sometimes result when leaders are in this age group, and workers primarily in the 26-40 age group. More about that in a moment. Chances are, the majority of the members of your church board come from this age group, although that may not be the case. In older, or more traditional congregations, most leaders may be over 55. In new church starts, and in younger congregations, the leadership will almost certainly be under 40. The leaders in the congregation will usually not only be the decision makers but the primary financial supporters as well.

This age group represents people born during the depression and war years. Births were lower in those years, and this group is considerably smaller than the 26-40 year olds. Many congregations are under-represented in this age group. That also creates interesting dynamics. When a congregation has few people in this age group, leadership goes either to an older or a younger group. That has important implications for a congregation's outreach ministry. Studies have shown that people born after World War II have major differences from those born earlier.[4] A number of those differences affect leadership. However, these differences are the result of factors so much a part of us we may not even recognize them. One potential result is tension between age groups arising from differences in attitudes and outlook.

An example of these differences, and their potential for creating tension, can be seen in the following comparison. People born between 1930-

1945 were born during times of hardship. Depression and a world war resulted in scarcity and shortages, and massive problems produced a climate of hardship. As a result, people born during this period are likely to face life with caution. They tend to be conservers, and to believe in delayed gratification. In contrast, people born during the years 1945-1960 were born in "boom times." They grew up in a society experiencing prosperity and growth, and the climate was one of optimism. As a result, people born during this period are likely to be risk-takers, who spend money easily, and who practice instant gratification.

Another factor may exist in congregations which have older leaders. There will be longer memories, and that can lead to the problem of "great yesterdays." The church was never more popular in this country than it was in the 1950s. Churches whose leadership is made up of people who were part of those golden years may have strong pressure to re-create them. That can, and often does, result in an attempt to use the same methods which worked then. When that situation exists, results are questionable and conflict is inevitable.

The solution to the problem of "great yesterdays" is "greater tomorrows." One of the tasks of leadership is to focus on what can be, and to plan for what will be. Leaders need to be future-oriented. They need to be workers as well.

Age 56-65 "Loyalists"

This group includes people who have been faithful and active members of the church for decades. Generally, they remain faithful and active; however, they are unlikely to be involved in the ministry efforts of the congregation in appreciable numbers. Many of them have spent years serving in various capacities, and they are more than happy to turn these responsibilities over to other (younger) people. These folks are enjoying the freedom of the "empty nest," and the benefits of leisure time and discretionary income. They prefer not to be tied down, as they enjoy weekends away or visits to children and grandchildren. When they are home they are in church. They continue to support the church faithfully. They are generally delightful people, who are strongly appreciative of their church and loyal to it.

Age 65 and above "Servant" and "Served"

Two categories are required to describe senior adults, and most people in this age group pass from one category to the other. All of us, to at least a degree, can put ourselves in one of these groups. For each of us it is at least in part a decision we make. Senior adults usually have the opportunity to choose to be "servants" until age and health factors remove the opportunity for choice.

Someone has said that the average American, upon reaching age 65, can anticipate thirteen additional years of health and vitality. During those years great opportunities for ministry exist, and since these people are usually retired they have time and energy for volunteer service. A beautiful opportunity for them is ministry to other senior adults.

This age group contains vast numbers of people both within and outside the church who deal with some of life's greatest difficulties: the loss of spouse and friends; loneliness; illness; the loss of capacity or opportunity to do things, and ultimately death. We need to work toward the development of intentional ministry to people dealing with these circumstances, and to facilitate that ministry being carried on by others in this group.

The task force will want to determine how many people in the congregation are in each age group. It will also be helpful to note particular groups within age-ranges which can be identified. This is especially important in considering the 26-40 age group. How many of the people our congregation has in this group are: parents of pre-school children? never married? divorced? part of a blended family? This identification will be most important in planning and implementing ministry efforts.

In one congregation of 200 members, the age ranges of the membership break down like this:

     18-25 — 12 people
     26-40 — 69 people
     41-55 — 39 people
     55-65 — 27 people
     65+   — 53 people

What conclusions would you begin to draw about ministry for a congregation whose age-ranges broke down in this way? Obviously, you will recognize the tremendous strength in the 26-40 bracket, and will be aware of potential for reaching that age group in society. You may also be conscious of the significant number of older adults. This congregation might well choose to have a second ministry focus on senior adults, and design program opportunities specifically designed for this group.

3. Review Your Average Worship Attendance

Not all congregations monitor worship attendance, but in reality it is one of the most important measurements. It is a much more accurate indication of a congregation's true size than any membership statistic. It is also crucial for monitoring growth and setting goals. Congregations seeking to attract worship visitors simply must keep at this to evaluate progress. Worship attendance should always be based on actual count, not estimate. An estimate of worship attendance is of no value.

For some congregations who have not been doing a count, the results will be painful. Many people have an inflated idea of the worship attendance of their congregation. When you estimate worship attendance, it's very easy to estimate too high. An actual count then, will likely be discouraging. But it is best to "bite the bullet" and do it. Once you know exactly where you are, you will be in a position to plan where you intend to go, and to measure progress along the way. Strict honesty in the count will benefit you in the long run.

If you compare average worship attendance over the past five years, you will be able to see exactly what progress you are making. The benefit is to look at what is happening in worship attendance over a period of years. One significant reason for doing that is that worship attendance tends to show up in membership figures two to five years later, since it usuaily takes that long for membership changes to be effected.

4. Assess the Strengths of Your Congregation

This may be determined in part by a sample poll of perhaps 10% of your membership. A brief questionnaire might be drawn up which asks:

- What do you most appreciate about this congregation?
- Which quality or activity of the church do you think would be most appealing to newcomers?
- What is your greatest source of satisfaction in this congregation?
- What attracted you to the church when you first came?

If you have a number of new members, a survey of them will be particularly useful. After all, their experience is fresh and will give the most accurate information about the strengths and weaknesses of your congregation's ministry with newcomers. You can use the questions above and formulate others. Some congregations include the question, "which members of the congregation did the most to make you feel welcome when you first came here?" This question is intended to identify and intentionally use the gifts of those who have particular effectiveness in this area.[5]

5. Analyze Your Present Ministries and the Volunteer Workers Who Participate In Them

We will deal with how to develop effective programs to attract visitors in a subsequent chapter, but two questions should be raised here. First, which current programs or ministries of your congregation are specifically designed and planned for unchurched people? The question is not intended to

have you identify programs or ministries in which
non-churched people may be included (one hopes
that all programs fit that description), but to identify
programs or ministries which have the
unchurched as their *primary focus.*

Our second question has a similar intent but
looks at the people you deploy in ministry. An early
and helpful contribution to understanding church
growth comes in the distinction between types of
workers in the church. The church's volunteer
workers may be divided into what are called class
one and class two workers. "Class one" workers
are the leaders whose energies are primarily directed *inward* toward the service of existing Christians and church structures. The contribution they
make is to serve those inside the church who
already believe. "Class two" workers are those
leaders whose energies are primarily directed
outward toward the unchurched. The contribution
they make is to serve those outside the church in
order to minister to their needs, encourage a response of faith, and invite them into the fellowship
of the church.

In most congregations, the overwhelming
majority of leaders are class one. It has been
suggested that in a congregation geared up for
growth, about one-quarter of the church's volunteer
pool should be class two workers.[6] The task force
will want to work out the present percentages for
your congregation.

Planning and Setting Goals for Evangelism

Having evaluated your community and
congregation, you are now ready to develop plans to
strengthen your outreach ministry, and to set goals
for the coming year. This is not a book about goal-

setting, so we will not deal with the process in detail. However, it may be that your task force will be asked to suggest some possible outreach goals to the governing board.

Goals are specific statements of intent, and the more definite they are, the easier it will be to address, monitor, and evaluate them. In his book on ratios, Win Arn suggests a number of possible areas in which outreach goals can be set. In the case of worship visitors, you might set goals for the improvement of your ministry with them. Dr. Arn suggests the need to work toward these goals:

- 25% of first-time visitors to eventually join, instead of the average 15%.
- One-third of first-time visitors return for a second visit, instead of the one-quarter which is about average.
- 75% of return visitors join the church, instead of the two-thirds which might ordinarily be anticipated.[7]

Many other goals could be set. Perhaps you will choose to set a goal for the number of new members you hope to attract in the coming year. Goals should be set which are realistic, and which will stretch you, and call for work and prayer. A possible goal might be to reach 50% more people than the average of the number received in the past two years, or perhaps a goal equal to ten, or even 15 percent of your total membership. Remember that the key is that the goal be both realistic and challenging. Just as goals are desirable in the area of increasing membership, so are they in terms of increasing worship attendance.

Another area in which planning and goal setting can take place is in programming to meet needs. Goals here might deal with specific efforts the congregation will undertake. A goal might be to begin six home Bible study groups, made up about equally of churched and non-churched persons, and to have 36 unchurched people actively participating. Another possibility would be to offer an eight week class on effective parenting on Thursday evenings in January and February, and to extend personal invitations to at least fifty non-churched persons.

Several suggestions about this task. First, it is important not to set more goals than can be handled. Probably three or four key goals are the most a congregation can manage. Second, it is crucial to have the active support of the congregation. (The term "active support" is used because you want more than just permission). A way needs to be found to have people in the congregation adopt and identify with the goals. The goals should energize and motivate the entire community. They need to be kept before the people, prayed for, reported on and rejoiced over. They are the congregation's goals. Third, no one group in the congregation should be seen as responsible for the goals. Every member of the congregation is called to help achieve them. That is why gifts have been given to each Christian. If, for example, the evangelism committee is assigned the task of monitoring the goals, their task should be seen not as working *on behalf of* the congregation to accomplish these results, but as working *through* the congregation to accomplish these results. Their task is to recruit, motivate, train, encourage, and deploy the congregation, as well as to assist the church to affirm and celebrate what God is doing.

Finally, once the goals are set, strategy needs to be developed to bring them to reality. If a goal is to increase average worship attendance by

15 percent, what means will be used to reach that goal? What will be done specifically to move toward the desired result? Ordinarily, several objectives will be drawn up for each goal. Possible objectives for a goal to increase worship attendance might include:

- to observe a Celebration of Friendship Sunday in April.
- To send two special mailings per month in January, February, and March to an area selected by the evangelism committee.
- To prepare a new brochure for the congregation, and to distribute 2,000 copies through the members.
- To conduct a "Come Home for Christmas," campaign in December to encourage the attendance of inactive members.

When objectives are approved, they need to be assigned to a committee so that the who, what, when, why, how, and where questions can be settled. After each event, the leadership team will want to evaluate the event and measure progress toward the goal.

We cannot be very effective in our outreach ministry until we know where we are, where we intend to be, and how we hope to get there. As we formulate a philosophy and strategy of outreach, and plan what we intend to do, we will be best able to evaluate the efforts of our congregation to share the good news of Jesus Christ, and welcome those who respond.

1 Roy M. Oswald and Speed B. Leas, *The Inviting Church* (Washington: The Alban Institute, 1987), p. 16.

2 *FOCUS*, p. 59.

3 Those interested in pursuing this matter are referred to two helpful studies written by Robert T. Gribbon and published by The Alban Institute: "When People Seek the Church" and "Half the Congregation: Ministry With 18—40 Year Olds." (Washington: The Alban Institute).

4 For a fascinating treatment of this matter, see Walrath, Douglas *Frameworks: Patterns of Living and Believing Today,* (Philadelphia: Pilgrim Press, 1987).

5 A sample of a new member survey is printed as Appendix A.

6 Win Arn, *The Church Growth Ratio Book* (Pasadena: Church Growth, Inc. 1987) p. 12.

7 *Ibid.*, p. 50.

Reflection Questions — Chapter Two

1. Over the past five years I think our congregation has been
    __ growing   __ declining   __ holding its own.

2. In my opinion, the majority of the new members our congregation receives have come because of
    __ the efforts of the pastor
    _ a program we offer
    __ publicity
    __ the invitation of a member.

3. As I look around on Sunday, it appears that the largest age group in worship is
    __ 0-18
    __ 18-25
    __ 26-40
    __ 41-55
    __ 56-65
    __ 65+

4. Our congregation has a planned strategy which involves a variety of methods of outreach.
    _ Yes   __ No   __ I have no idea

5. In my opinion, the unchurched people who live within driving distance of our church would probably represent the following percentage of the population.
    __ Under 10%
    __ 10-25%
    __ 26-40%
    __ 40% or more

6. As I look around on Sunday, it would appear that we have first time visitors
    __ every Sunday

   _ Most of the time
   _ Occasionally
   _ Hardly ever

7. It seems to me that if a visitor attends a service in our church, he/she
   _ is almost certain to return
   _ will probably return
   _ would be unlikely to return.

8. I am personally aware that our church has
   _ an up-to-date purpose statement
   _ an identified target group
   _ a clearly defined ministry area
   _ a list of current goals
   _ at least one program addressed to unchurched people.

9. How would you respond if someone asked you what you most value about your church?

10. What is the age of the majority of the leaders in your congregation?
   _ Under 40
   _ 40-55
   _ Over 55

What implications does your answer suggest?
As you reflect on these questions, which areas do you believe need to be addressed most urgently in your church?

1.
2.
3.
4.

If you were to help your congregation make a new beginning in one area, which would it be?

Three Steps for Attracting the First-Time Visitor

A first-time visitor enters your church for Sunday worship. What has brought him/her? Can we identify the probable factor, or factors, responsible for this person's arrival on this particular Lord's Day? What is it which attracts the first-time visitor?

Three steps for seeing your first-time visitor rate increase will be presented, each of which supports and reinforces the others. We will introduce them in the way they might be experienced by a non-churched person from the community, although the three steps are listed in the reverse order of their importance and effectiveness.

STEP ONE: ADVERTISING

Advertising alone will not produce growth, but it can be an important ingredient in the mix. Lyle Schaller points out that a congregation serious about growth will spend a minimum of five percent of its budget on advertising.[1]

One benefit of advertising is that it enables your congregation to become known in the community. The Alban Institute study on *The Inviting Church* [2] reports a survey of new members which asked the question "How did you first become aware of this church?" Fifty-seven percent of those responding were told about the church by someone. Seven percent saw an advertisement. Two conclusions can be drawn: word of mouth is by far the most effective kind of advertising, and paid advertisements do have some impact.

1. The Church Sign

We shall return to word of mouth advertising later, but for now let us consider the more formal methods of advertising. Possibly the single most important advertising a church can do is through the sign it has in front of its building. The survey mentioned above indicated that 30 percent of the newcomers who joined the church came because they noticed the church when they were in the neighborhood. I wonder how many of them responded to the church's sign?

In his book on church advertising, Steve Dunkin offers helpful advice on this subject.[3] He recommended that churches:
a) Put up a sign that is perpendicular to the road. This will require you to print on both sides of the sign, but will allow the sign to be read by people driving by in either direction. That is essential, since far more people are likely to drive by than walk past your building.

b) Make it readable. Have it large enough to be read easily, and put it as close to the road as you can.

c) Make it legible. Use large letters and plain lettering. The aim is not to be artistic, but clear.

d) Keep the sign simple. A simple and plain design is likely to be most effective, and brief messages can be readily absorbed.

e) In addition to the church's name and times of worship and Sunday School, include a descriptive phrase which sets forth an essential quality of the congregation. A church I drove past last winter had this message on its sign: "A warm church for cold days."

In addition to advertising through the sign on the property, several other methods may be mentioned. If your church building is not located on a main thoroughfare, it will be helpful to erect directional signs on a main traffic artery, if that is permissible. Some denominations have signs available for purchase. Anyone who has spent time looking for a particular church can attest to the feeling of gratitude such a sign will produce.

2. The Yellow Pages

An advertisement in the Yellow Pages is effective in reaching new residents who may be looking for a church. Market research indicates that people under age 40 use the Yellow Pages frequently. A wise approach is to take as large an ad as possible, and include both your advertising theme and a brief reference to any specific ministries your congregation offers.

3. Mailings

Mailings have been used effectively in some congregations. Effectiveness grows with a) the frequency of your mailings (a minimum of six should be planned); b) the focus of your mailings (the more specific your target group, the better advertising results will be). Some congregations develop a strategy of six mailings in a year to a specific postal zipcode area or geographical zone in their ministry area. Generally, each mailing has two items included. A plan for a year of mailings might follow the following format:

• January — An introductory letter is sent bringing greetings from the congregation and indicating your desire to share information about the church. It is a letter of welcome and invitation and a well-designed brochure introducing the congregation is included.

• February or March — A mailing goes out about the church's schedule of Lenten observances, and specifically invites attendance at the Easter service. A brief message about the meaning and significance of Easter is included.

• April — A letter of invitation to a prospective member's class is mailed out the week before Easter. The class will begin the Sunday after Easter. The invitation is written in such a way as to encourage the attendance of those who wish to know more about following Jesus. The letter makes clear that no pressure for decision will occur. This mailing includes an attractive flyer containing an invitation to the Easter services.

• July — An invitation to a church social event is mailed. Perhaps the congregation invites the community for ice cream sundaes on the church lawn.   Information about the congregation's Bible Study groups is included.

• Early September — An invitation to come to church following summer vacation is sent, along with a brochure about educational opportunities, classes, and other events which will begin in the fall.

• November or December— A special mailing goes out inviting people to the Christmas service. A new brochure about the congregation is included.

We have suggested including a brochure in a mailing about your congregation. A well written and attractive brochure introducing your congregation is an excellent advertisement for your church.

Many brochures make the mistake of saying too much. People are unlikely to read long sections of print.   Use pictures, a good logo, and an attractive design. Include pictures of people. An effective approach is to print pictures of some of your members along with a one sentence statement about what the church means to them. For the content of the rest, you need, of course, to give basic information about the schedule and to introduce the pastor. In addition, the brochure should highlight two things: *what you offer*, in terms of need-meeting ministry; and *who you are*, which is communicated through a descriptive phrase or two which describes essential characteristics of your congregation.

4. Newspaper Advertising

Some churches place advertisements on the church page of the local newspaper each week. There may be good reasons for that, but no congregation should fool itself into thinking that such advertising will reach the unchurched. Very few unchurched people read that part of the paper, and none are likely to show up because they are intrigued by the sermon title. The church-page advertisement may attract travelers, may reach some new residents who are believers and are looking for a new church home, and might draw someone who is dissatisfied with his present congregation. Generally speaking, the congregation which advertises on the church page does so primarily for the sake of its own members. That is fine, as long as it is recognized. Incidentally, it may well be true that the church which regularly advertises will have more success in getting favorable treatment on news releases which highlight significant events. That is an important consideration, since that kind of publicity can be very valuable.

Newspaper advertising designed to reach the unchurched is quite different. It will be planned to run in the section of the paper most likely to be read by the people to whom the message is addressed. The day on which it will run will be carefully selected. For example, it has been suggested that Monday is an ideal day for a reflective advertisement, because of the need many people seem to have for something to brighten that day and because it may help someone to recognize the emptiness of a wasted weekend.

Advertising to reach the unchurched does not have as its primary goal getting people to come to the worship service, but rather enabling them to recognize needs and to understand that their needs are addressed by your church. Two types of messages fit this criterion. One is what we might call a reflective advertisement. The purpose is to help people think about life. Here is an example:

"I have come that you might have life . . .
      life in all its fullness."   Jesus
Have you experienced that life?
Perhaps we can discover it together.
Join us at: Christ Community Church
Washington at Central
Telephone Number: 285-4600

An advertisement like this is designed to help people reflect on the meaning and purpose of life. It suggests that we all need to experience the presence of Christ and his significance for our lives. It offers the ministry of the church in a servant role, and does not infer that Christians have solved all of life's problems. It communicates the message that Jesus Christ is the key to experiencing the fullness of life.

A second type of advertising to reach the unchurched addresses a specific need, and offers a concrete response. For example, an advertisement might be addressed to recently divorced persons and indicate the formation of a divorce recovery group. Another possibility is to address a common need such as loneliness and indicate as specifically as possible how your congregation ministers to this need.

Some congregations run this kind of advertisement in the "personals" column. Another strategy is to run the ad very visibly, with more "white space" than words. Newspaper advertising can be very effective in small to fairly large cities. It is not very helpful in large metropolitan areas, largely because of cost and diversity of coverage. In some communities a local shopper's paper can be used with effectiveness. In our community in the Chicago area for example, in addition to receiving one of the major Chicago papers, many people receive a regional community newspaper which may be published once or twice weekly. Such a paper can be an excellent medium for your congregation's advertising, since it is read by the people who live in your church's ministry area.

5. Radio and Television Advertising

Radio and television advertising are sometimes utilized effectively, although they can be expensive. A number of churches in the Reformed Church in America have had excellent results from a brief advertisement which immediately follows, and identifies with, Robert Schuller's "Hour of Power" telecast. The effectiveness of that approach seems to depend, to a considerable degree, on the area where the advertising congregation is located. Also, effectiveness is diminished when more than one congregation is featured in the advertisement. Apparently church advertising does not lend itself well to being a cooperative venture.

Churches should be particularly conscious of the opportunity to communicate their message during the Christmas and Easter seasons, and should develop a planned advertising program to take advantage of the openness of people to a spiritual message in these times. Those interested in a further exploration of media use for the church are referred to a helpful study by Theodore Baehr.[4]

STEP TWO: PROGRAMMING

If the question is, "What do we advertise?" the answer is often, "our church's program." The second step in attracting visitors is through the programs the church provides. Several principles are key. Program is most effective when:

1. *It is provided for all age groups*

A congregation should provide programs for all age groups. Smaller membership churches will need to be creative here, since their resources are limited, and they may have "gaps" in some age groups. The point is that if some age groups are left out of the church's program, the potential for attracting new members is restricted. A parent is unlikely to join a congregation which offers no activity for a teen-aged son. The small membership church may need to carry out some aspects of its program in cooperation with another congregation. While there are disadvantages in that, at least for church growth, it is far better to offer something, than to have nothing.

2. *It is broadly based*

Provide a wide variety of programs. If we think of programs as "entry points" it will be easy to recognize that the greater the number of entry points, the greater the number of people who will be attracted. Congregations need to stretch themselves to continue to develop new programs. It may be possible to begin a new Bible study group; to sponsor a new athletic team; to offer a new type of senior adult program. Each year the congregation should seek to add at least one new program — the goal being to increase the number of events and activities to which people can be invited.

3. *It is of high quality*

Provide quality programs. To be effective in making a positive impact, programs offered must be done well. If newcomers attend an ill-conceived and poorly conducted program they will be unfavorably impressed and resistant to future attempts to reach them. Congregations are wise to offer only as much program as can be done well. That requires careful planning and concerted effort. To do one new program each year, and do it well, is a good goal.

4. It is specifically and intentionally designed to reach the unchurched

A church in Kalamazoo, Michigan reserves Thursday evenings on its calendar for programs designed to reach the unchurched. Groups and organizations in the congregation schedule events on that night only if their prime purpose is outreach. There may be a film series, or a class for new parents, or a Bible study group, but whatever is planned is designed primarily for people who are not members of the church. A church in Minneapolis has regularly scheduled golf outings as a means of attracting unchurched men. To participate, a foursome must include two men who are not from the church (or from any church, one hopes). Two men in the congregation sign up for a slot, and each brings an unchurched friend. After a round of golf, a meal is served and socializing continues. Friendships are formed, connections with the church established, and new people come into the church.

5. It is specifically directed to your target audience

In planning new programming efforts, a congregation will want to be sure that it responds to the needs and interests of the group it has identified as its primary target audience. If that group is senior adults, for example, the congregation will have identified needs in that population group to which it can respond programmatically, and set in place some program or ministry designed specifically for that group.

Program Development and Leadership

How are programs developed? Robert Schuller is fond of saying "Find a need and fill it." Needs are most readily identified by people out of their own life experiences. Often needs will emerge from the congregation. In a church I formerly served, we became aware that four active members of the congregation were all battling cancer. Out of the experience of those cancer patients and their families came first a growing awareness of this area of need, and second, a decision to form a cancer support group as a means of ministry to the community.

An excellent strategy for program development was born out of that experience. It has been refined somewhat since we first "discovered" it, and can be utilized for any church program. It begins with the selection of a core group who will develop the program. These are people among whom the idea originated, or who are chosen because they share the need to which the program responds. Four people are needed as a minimum to make the method effective. If the program is planned for a specific age group, all four will be in that age group. If it is a program which addresses a need, the people chosen are those who themselves share that need. This is essential. Thus, a divorce recovery group is created by people who have been divorced, and a new parents class is designed by new parents.

In accepting leadership for the new program, the core group accepts responsibility for five tasks:

Planning Since they know the needs to which the program will respond, they are the ones who need to plan it. In addition to content and format, planning also will address the length of and the arrangements for the proposed program.

Participation Members of the core group make a commitment to attend each session.

Inviting and recruiting A significant life experience invariably brings us into contact with other people who share that experience. That provides natural opportunities to extend invitations. The core group accepts responsibility for gathering participants. In some cases, members of the core group agree to bring at least two others, thus assuring an attendance of at least 12 people at the first session.

Hosting Serving as host involves a variety of tasks and is usually alternated among the core group. It means coming early to prepare the room, getting refreshments ready, and welcoming people as they arrive. It means staying late to talk with anyone who lingers, as well as cleaning up and closing up when the meeting has concluded. The primary concern in hosting, however, is the people, not the place.

Following-up Group sessions and informal conversations will often reveal information about particular needs, such as transportation or child care. Members of the core group respond to those needs by making arrangements for someone to help out. Follow-up includes contacting participants who are absent, and providing for a process by which the congregation can continue to minister to the person when the group has completed its life.

Some programs for unchurched people have a brief focus, some last longer, but all have an announced schedule with a definite termination. Each is designed to enable people to experience the love and support of the Christian community. If a program is not effectively accomplishing that, or if it is not reaching the people for whom it is designed, the program should be terminated. There need be no guilt in such a decision.

STEP THREE: INVITING

Far and away the single most important aspect of a congregation's ability to attract new members is the degree to which members invite others. Probably the best known church growth statistic has been identified by Church Growth, Inc., which indicates that between 75-90% of all adults who join a congregation are first brought by a friend or relative.[5] There is no more effective method of church growth than the personal invitations extended by church members.

The best resource I know of to enable this to happen is THE MASTER'S PLAN "Church Action Kit" which has been produced by Church Growth, Inc.[6] In using this teaching/learning resource, members of the congregation are helped to identify and intentionally reach out to members of their "extended family." The course provides training in friendship evangelism. Church Growth, Inc. has also produced a planning kit for a special "Celebration Sunday," which is a designated Sunday for members to invite an unchurched friend or relative to the worship service.[7]

Lyle Schaller describes the characteristics of congregations who do well in inviting others. "The congregations in which the members invite others to come to church with them usually display these characteristics: (a) the members are enthusiastic about their faith as Christians, (b) the members are enthusiastic about this congregation, (c) the members are enthusiastic about the current pastor, (d) the congregation as a whole conveys the expectation that members will invite others to come to church with them, (e) most of the members actively and enthusiastically greet and welcome visitors, and (f) that particular program or, if it is on Sunday morning, that worship experience is planned on the assumption that first-time visitors will be present. This means minimizing references to 'last week,' to congregation problems, to administrative concerns or to 'in house' jokes that leave the stranger mystified."[8]

Earlier we suggested that the three parts of the strategy support and enhance one another. Advertising commends and announces program. Program provides opportunity for inviting. Invitations are extended to people who have seen an advertisement. Churches hoping to attract new members will work for the improvement of their congregation's effort in all three areas.

1 Lyle Schaller: "Where Are the Visitors?", (Church Management — The Clergy Journal, April 1984), p. 147.

2 Roy M. Oswald and Speed B. Leas, *The Inviting Church* (Washington: The Alban Institute, 1987), p. 28.

3 Steve Dunkin, *Church Advertising: A Practical Guide,* (Nashville: Abingdon Press, 1982) pp. 104, 105.

4 Theodore Baehr, *Getting the Word Out,* (New York: Harper and Row, 1986).

5 Arn, The Master's Plan, p. 43.

6 The kit is available from Church Growth, Inc. 2670 S. Myrtle Ste. #201, Monrovia, CA 91016.

7 More information on this strategy will be found in Chapter Six.

8 Lyle Schaller: "Where Are the Visitors?" (Church Management — The Clergy Journal, April 1984), p. 147.

Reflection Questions — Chapter Three

1. Our church spends the following percentage of the budget on advertising:
    __ 0-2%   __ 2-5%   __ 5-10%

2. Our church sign is:
    __ Woefully inadequate
    __ So-So
    __ Just about perfect

3. Our church has an attractive, up-to-date brochure which is regularly distributed.
    __ Yes   __ No

4. Our church has a committee which plans and reviews our advertising strategy.
    __ Yes   __ No

5. Our church regularly offers programs designed primarily to reach unchurched people.
    __ Yes   __ No

6. Our church offers quality programs for all age groups.   __ Yes   __ No

7. Our church has started at least one new program in the past year. __ Yes __ No

8. Our church has a strategy for developing new programs as needs are identified.
    __ Yes __ No

9. Members of our congregation regularly being their friends to church. __ Yes __ No

10. Our church offers training in friendship evangelism through a planned on-going program.   __ Yes __ No

Of the questions to which you answered "No", which seems most urgent to address?

How would you get started?

What Visitors Are
Looking For

While it is sometimes difficult for visitors to entirely understand why they feel a certain way about a church, at least after the first one or two visits, their attitude — and decision to return — is generally a result of six factors. They are listed here in their probable order of importance. However, all of them interact in the reactions of visitors to your church, and all play a role in a person's decision about affiliation.

1. The Friendliness and Warmth of the Church.

In his book *How to Build A Magnetic Church,* Herb Miller quotes Warren J. Hartman, research director for the United Methodist Church, who says: "When both unchurched and churched people are asked what they look for in a church ...

all of them agree about one factor — the climate of the congregation. They are looking for a church in which they feel at home, where the people are friendly, and where there is a warm and comfortable atmosphere."[1] The warmth and friendliness of the congregation are probably the most important characteristics of congregations effective in attracting new members.

Possibly you have been a member of your present church long enough to have difficulty remembering what it was like for you the first time you attended, but perhaps you do recall being on vacation and attending an unfamiliar congregation. Do you remember how awkward and self-conscious you felt? Yet, as an active church member, you were coming into the church more like a relative than a stranger. If you, who are comfortable attending church, felt self-conscious when visiting another congregation, imagine what it must be like for someone to come to your worship service who has never attended church, or has been away from it for a long time. It must be very difficult for that visitor. It is our responsibility to make that visitor's experience as pleasant for him or her as we can, just as if he or she were a guest in our home.

It is not easy for church members to be accurate in their assessment of the warmth and friendliness of their congregation. In all probability, our church feels warm and friendly to us. (If it does not, we probably will not be there very long.) But how warm and friendly does it appear to a newcomer? One way to discover that is to ask our newcomers. Another way is to determine how many of our first time visitors return. If the return rate is less than 25 percent, it may be an indication that the congregation is not as warm and friendly as it should be.

At what point in their visit would first-time visitors feel most uncomfortable? It is 1) when they first enter the building, and 2) when the formal part of the service is over and people begin to leave. These are two important moments we need to consider.

Many congregations deal with the first need by having greeters located at the door through which visitors enter the building. This, by the way, is much more effective than placing greeters at the entrance to the worship area. Greeters need to be selected on the basis of relational skills and trained in their responsibilities. An essential element in the training is to enable the greeters to understand that they are there for the visitor. Members enjoy being greeted, but it is not essential to greet them. It is essential to greet visitors.

Ideally, greeters will recognize those who are not members. A training session can help a greeter know how to deal with someone when the greeter is uncertain whether the person is a visitor or an unrecognized member. The best approach is to assume the person is a visitor, and greet the person with warmth. Suggested approaches are for the greeter to introduce himself and say something like, "I don't believe we have met, have we?" or even, "I have been coming here for two years, how about you?"

The greeting of visitors should be neither rushed nor gushy. Too much attention can be as uncomfortable as too little. When a first time visitor has been identified, ideally the greeter would introduce him or her to a member who is near, who would offer to accompany the visitor to the worship area, and introduce the visitor to an usher. If that is not practicable, the greeter will at least give directions, and ask the visitor if he or she needs any further assistance.

The warmth and friendliness of the congregation will be judged by the visitor primarily on the basis of how many people spoke to him or her. Greeters fill an important function before the service. Even so, their friendliness is seen as part of their job, and the welcome of one individual member who comes up to the visitor to greet him or her will have more impact than the most gracious welcome of an official greeter.

Secondly, we need to consider what happens after worship. Entering the sanctuary may be thought of as an individual act since people do it more or less separately. Even so, churches usually have ushers to help in the process. Leaving the sanctuary is a group experience, since we do it together. This can be the loneliest moment of all, if everyone is greeting friends, while the visitor goes up the aisle in a pocket of isolated silence. And now, no usher is available to ease the visitor's discomfort.

The primary way of dealing with this matter is by helping your members understand the need for them to approach, and welcome, anyone they do not recognize, or anyone who appears to be alone. Almost everyone can learn to do that, and to carry on a conversation as they walk up the aisle.

Many churches have a pastor or church leader at the exit from the sanctuary. This person greets worshippers as they leave. While this is a good practice, it does not provide a meaningful way to respond to visitors. It is either a busy and rushed time or someone stops to talk and other people begin to slip by. A better way to respond to visitors following worship is to have four or five people (for typical congregation of about 200) assigned to function as "unofficial" greeters. Here is how the method works.

The members selected for this task must have good hospitality skills. These people can be selected from among those whom newcomers have identified as having made them feel most welcome. Or, you can poll your members and ask them which people in the church do the most effective job of welcoming visitors.

If enough people are recruited, several teams of 4-6 people are drawn up, and one team is assigned for each Sunday. Their job is to mingle, and look for visitors or people who seem to be ignored by others. They may function both before and after worship, although as we have suggested, the latter is more important. These "minglers" simply try to intentionally welcome visitors and convey friendliness to them. In the overall visitor strategy, they will perform a vital task.

The greater the number of people who greet the visitors, the more certain the visitor is about the friendliness and warmth of the congregation. I recently read in a church newsletter the story of a man who visited 18 churches on consecutive Sundays to discover how friendly they were to newcomers. In each visit, the man followed the same pattern. He always sat near the front so he would exit the length of the sanctuary. When possible, he re-entered the sanctuary and exited by another aisle. Before leaving, he would approach someone and ask for directions to the men's room. He devised the following rating scale:

A smile of welcome	10 points
A word of greeting	10 points
Exchange of names	100 points

Invitation to return	200 points
Introduction to another member	1000 points
An invitation to meet the pastor	2000 points

In 11 of the 18 churches visited, less than 100 points were scored; in five churches fewer than 20. The point to recognize is that when visitors feel that no one cares whether or not they have come, they are not likely to return.

Probably never before has the warmth and friendliness of a local church been more important. Vast numbers of people are living at a distance from the community in which they grew up. Many live far from other relatives. Loneliness seems universal. Psychologists point out that the most frequent problems with which they deal spring from a lack of meaningful relationships. The love and friendship implicitly promised in the gospel must be experienced by worship visitors in the welcome they receive when they visit our churches.

2. The Character of the Worship Service

A study of new members in The Christian Church (Disciples of Christ) revealed that 82.7 percent of new members rated the quality of the worship service as an important reason for joining.[2] While those results might not be duplicated elsewhere, it is unquestionably true that the worship service is a key ingredient in determining whether a person will respond positively to the prospect of becoming affiliated with that church.

Congregations that provide programming which addresses a variety of needs will find that for many people, the first visit to a church building will be to attend a program, class, or other event. Still, one supposes, for the great majority of people who become members of a congregation, the first visit made to church is for worship. That makes the character of the worship experience highly important.

What are the issues to consider in reflecting on the character of the worship? Several questions will help us examine this issue.

Is it authentic? Perhaps you are dissatisfied that the first question raised seems so subjective and imprecise. The reason is that newcomers who have been asked about the worship seem to have difficulty describing what they wish to convey. That may be because most of us have difficulty accurately describing spiritual matters. It may also be that what newcomers are looking for is easier to sense than to describe. What people want in worship is integrity and meaning. They want the worship service to enable them to experience the presence of God. They hope to hear a word from God. They are looking for clarity and guidance to know what is right, and for motivation and power to do the right. They hope to be lifted above themselves, to see a vision of a better world, of themselves as better people. Hope, acceptance, strength are desired. Is the worship real, or is it just for show?

Does it echo with the notes of grace? People who come to church for worship need to hear — loudly and clearly — the accent of grace. In my view, people who come to worship — churched and unchurched alike — already know that they are sinners. They don't need to be convinced of that. What they doubt, or cannot believe, is the reality and depth of God's love for them. That note of grace needs to be struck again and again, so that it echoes throughout the worship service, and is still ringing in the worshipper's ears on the way home.

I have often asked people "If you could hear God say one thing to you, what do you think it would be?" Invariably people suggest that God would come with a rebuke: "Why don't you pray more?" or "You need to try harder." That is not my view. I believe God would come to you, put his arm around you, and say, "Do you know how much I love you?" Isn't that, after all, what the ministry of Jesus was all about?

Worship must communicate grace, not only as the content of what happens, but the context as well. Grace must be not only proclaimed, but expressed; not simply spoken, but seen. In planning worship, leaders should keep in mind this question: "What is the good news the congregation will experience through this service?"

Is the worship designed to include everyone? Some years ago, my wife and I attended church in an area where we were vacationing. No printed order of worship was available, but there were numerous responses used, and we had no idea what was happening. We felt so out of place we wished we had not come. That may seem an extreme example, but many people have had an experience like it. We need to do all we can to enable visitors to feel comfortable. They are honored guests.

A number of things can be done to help visitors feel included. A cordial welcome can be given them, both verbally and in a printed bulletin. Doing this at every service will not only touch the lives of visitors, but will do something for the congregation as well, including creating the expectation that visitors are anticipated at every service. Another suggestion is to print in full any responses which are to be said or sung by the congregation. If the worship leader "reads" the familiar words the people recite, it will help the visitor, who does not know them, to feel less self-conscious about reading them.

Inclusion is also communicated through the content, language, and leadership of the worship. Inclusive language; examples and illustrations which include women and children; the encouragement and recognition of the presence of children in worship; the use of a variety of worship leaders, including women and youth; provision of a barrier-free building; all these communicate that your congregation is open to all, and the full participation of each person is valued.

Is the worship celebrative? Joy is an essential element in worship, and one hopes it will come through clearly. Worship is meant to be an uplifting experience that enables people to leave the service strengthened and equipped for life. The hope is that worshippers will be able to identify with the psalmist who reported: "I was glad when they said to me, 'Let us go to the house of the Lord'" (Psalm 122:1). Joy is communicated, at least in part, by the attitude and expression of those who lead worship.

Other worship issues. In a chapter on worship, Herb Miller identifies a number of additional issues which might be considered in evaluating the impact of the worship service on the visitor. We will simply list some of them. Miller's book can be consulted for those who wish to pursue the matter further.[3] He advocates:

- The sharing of the joys and concerns of the congregation.

- A worship style appropriate to the region or environment of the congregation.
- Variety in worship.
- Bright cheerful music.
- Singing familiar hymns.
- Lively preaching.

3. A Family Place for Children

This is the third crucial component in the requirements for a congregation wishing to attract new members. In 1986, what was then the American Lutheran Church reported the results of a study conducted in their denomination. The study asked new members why they had joined the church. The answer most often given (by 49.5 percent of those surveyed), was "for the sake of the children."[4] In the study The Alban Institute carried out, people also identified the needs of their children as a major factor in the decision to seek out the church.[5]

The sheer number of persons who gave this answer is an indication that new church members are likely to be in the baby-boom generation. The baby-boom generation generally represents people in the 26-40 age group. This is the largest group of adults in the population, and in fact, the baby-boom generation, those people born between the years of 1946-1964, includes one-third of the American people. You might find it helpful to go back to page 17 and review what was written there about this age group.

It will come as no surprise that parents want moral and spiritual values taught to their children, and that this is a high priority for them. In fact, many people seek out the church at the time when they have children or when they are ready for religious instruction. They are looking for congregations that provide effective ministry to children. Religious education classes, youth groups, and other occasions for ministry to and with children and young people have always been valued. Their importance is probably even greater now, since public schools, for a variety of reasons, cannot fulfill this function.

In a previous generation it might have been a grandparent or another member of the extended family who helped provide spiritual and moral training for children. In our time, when many people live apart from other relatives, no member of an extended family is available to give such instruction. Many parents feel they have neither the time nor the skills to take on the task. The church is looked to as the place children can receive this instruction. The congregation needs to respond by providing effective educational opportunities for children and youth. Those churches who do so will be effective in outreach.

4. The Adult Program

During the 1950s and early '60s a prevailing view in the church was that if a church could reach children in the community through an attractive educational program, the parents would follow and make their way into the church. Unfortunately, it rarely worked that way. Parents would show up for a program which featured their children, but did not keep coming. It is important that we remember this in order to avoid repeating the mistake.

As important as religious education for their children is to many parents, an excellent children's educational program will not be enough to bring parents into the church. And obviously for adults who are not parents or whose children are grown, it will have no effect. Congregations wanting to reach unchurched adults also need to provide quality adult programs. Adult education is a vital element in a congregation's outreach program.

Adult education is desired by and important to vast numbers of adults. Bible study groups are particularly opportune. I heard George Gallup give an address in which he indicated his belief that small group Bible studies for adults provide the greatest evangelistic opportunity today. The American public is fascinated with the person of Jesus, and a class or group to study Christ's life and teachings will always have a place. We are a society which remains interested in "how to do it" questions, and many people are looking for help and growth in areas such as marriage enrichment, effective parenting, managing grief, and even understanding Islam. Classes offered by congregations which are designed to include unchurched people, and for which specific invitations are given, will be an effective aid to an outreach ministry.

Another opportunity for involving un-churched adults is to offer ministry opportunities in which unchurched adults can participate. A church in England, wishing to involve members of its community, asked people in the church's neighborhood what they felt was the most pressing need in the community. When the responses were tabulated, a specific need was identified. The people who had suggested that need were then contacted by the congregation and invited to participate in the church's attempt to minister to that need. Every community has needs. It might be possible for your congregation to begin a program such as the rehabilitating of a house; teaching remedial reading; providing food for hunger relief; or establishing a group to visit people in prison. You might offer study groups which focus on a specific area of concern such as hunger relief or prison reform which could be springboards for ministry.

Other activities which the congregation offers for adults can also be part of an outreach program. Athletic events or classes, musical groups, exercise or fitness groups, and social gatherings can all be designed to include unchurched people. Members can be encouraged to extend invitations to their friends and relatives. People from outside the church who come for such an event or activity may meet and establish friendships with persons presently involved in the life of the congregation and be encouraged to participate in other aspects of the church's life.

Adult education offers ongoing opportunities for ministry which ought to be recognized. Many adults are eager for substantive learning. A planned curriculum offering in-depth Bible study will attract persons who have a serious interest in spiritual growth. Mission-outreach opportunities, such as participating in a Habitat for Humanity housing project, will also attract interested adults. The more adult activities you offer, the more doors through which people may come into your church.

5. The Church Building

Unless your congregation is at the point of constructing a new facility, you probably cannot do much about your building. Your location, and your structure, are fixed, and therefore, not a factor you can change in your visitor attraction strategy.

True? Only partially. It is important to understand what it is about your church facility which attracts or deters visitors because there may be some things which can be corrected and some things for which you must compensate. Here are four key questions:

A. *Is your church visible?* The more visible your building, church growth experts say, the greater your growth potential. If your church building is located on a side street, in a low traffic area, or is hidden from view, you need to compensate. Advertising becomes more important. Directional signs from the nearest thoroughfare are desirable. Print a map on your church brochure. A good example of compensating is a church in a hard-to-find location that printed and distributed a quantity of attractive brochures. Prominently featured was a map with directions. Accompanying the map was this statement: "We are a church that is hard to find but worth the effort."

B. *Is your church accessible?* It is, of course, important that your building be accessible to handicapped people. If it isn't, it would be well for the church to determine whether changes can be made which would facilitate the participation of such persons. But accessibility is also an issue for others. Do people who first come to your church know where to enter? Some churches keep the main entrance doors locked, because "no one comes in that way." What about the first-time visitor? Will he or she find the church accessible? Accessibility may not even occur to your members as an issue, and yet be a barrier to a first-time visitor.

C. *What is the condition of your property?* Many congregations meet in older buildings and find maintenance to be an ongoing and perhaps unsolvable problem. This is an especially difficult situation for many city churches, not a few of whom find themselves trying to manage the upkeep of old buildings in an area of high prices and poor people. It will not do to pretend there are easy answers here.

Having said that, however, let us recognize that some things can be done about the condition of the building. For one thing, it can be kept clean and neat. Relatively little money is required to keep a building looking warm and inviting. Cleanliness is crucial. And the three most important areas are, in order: the nursery, rest rooms and kitchen.   A friend told me that, as a new resident, he and his family visited a neighborhood church. They liked some things about it very much but never went back for a second visit because they were unhappy about the condition of the nursery. Any congregation serious about growth will take care to provide the best possible nursery facilities.

The sanctuary can also be made to look attractive. Cheerful colors, inviting posters, artistic banners all help commend the congregation.   A tended lawn, shrubbery, a good coat of paint are important in a first impression. Whatever the church has can be dressed up and made to look its best. A well cared for and attractively decorated building communicates a positive message about the people who worship there, and adds its own invitation and welcome to those who approach it.

D. Do you have adequate space? Church growth experts point out that when your worship attendance reaches the point that your sanctuary is consistently at 85 percent of capacity, it begins to be a hindrance to further growth. Many people hesitate to attend a service they expect will be uncomfortably full. The prevailing wisdom is that when you reach the 85 percent of capacity level, it is time to start the process for adding an additional service. There may be some people who object that a second service will cause a loss of fellowship among the members, but good arguments can be advanced for a second service. One point to recognize is that it allows for added variety in that one service can be planned to be different. A more important reason is that adding an additional service almost always increases total attendance. The most important rebuttal is that fellowship should never come at the expense of a loss of outreach to new people.

The same points can be made about educational facilities. If you have the wonderful problem of overcrowded Sunday School classes, add a second session. It will mean more teachers need to be recruited and trained — and that does take work — but it also results in more people involved. Parking space may also be a problem. If you have inadequate parking, and are unable to do much about it, a good approach is to reserve the best spaces for visitors, and put up signs indicating "Visitor's Parking." If those spaces are unoccupied, the congregation should be helped to see that more visitors need to be invited.

6. The Church's Image

What is the image your church has among the people of your community? Three possibilities exist: It has none, it has a negative image, it has a positive image. Only one is good. A positive image will be an asset for a congregation seeking to attract

new members. No image will not attract visitors.
A negative image will keep them away.

While not easy, it is possible to create or
improve the image of your congregation. By far the
most effective way is through a need-meeting
ministry in the community. We have probably all
heard accounts of a church whose building
sustains no damage in an area where other
buildings have been vandalized. The building is
preserved because people recognize a congregation
which serves. A ministry meeting a real need in
the community is a guaranteed method of
generating a positive image for the church.

Building usage for community groups will
also enhance the image of the church. Making
your facility available to the community is a proven
way to generate goodwill. It is a practical demonstration of servanthood, the model to which we are
called. People often ask if making the building
available to community groups will contribute to
church growth. The answer is "not directly." Very
few people join a church simply because they go to
an aerobics class that meets there. Yet if that class
has members of the congregation who winsomely
relate to, and extend invitations to unchurched
participants, you have an excellent potential for
growth. Making your facility available has a
positive effect on a church's image.

A third way to improve image is through
pastoral visibility. This happens when the pastor
attends community functions, participates in civic
groups and community activities, attends high
school events, and is visible in and available to the
community. Some pastors make it known that
ministerial services are available to the
community. A church board needs to explore this
issue so an understanding can be reached about the

time the pastor spends in the community. When no agreement has been reached on this matter, there may be resentment among some members about the use of the pastor's time. Church leaders have a key role in establishing the principle that pastors are part of what the church offers the community.

Publicity can also impact the image of a church. Unfortunately, negative publicity is often dominant. Nothing seems to travel faster than stories of pastoral or congregational folly. But good publicity can also be generated. The best kind arises naturally from a positive ministry. You can't buy a news story in which the church is featured in the local paper, but a unique program or ministry may generate response from the local paper. Selfless acts of service which are unusually creative or generous may be reported by the media to the wider community. Take the initiative in alerting the local media and the publicity will give a powerful boost to the congregation's image.

A church interested in being recognized and in improving its image, will want a publicity committee. One task of such a group is to submit news releases about programs and ministries of the church. Baehr's book will be helpful to those interested in exploring ways to carry out the task.[6]

Another task for the publicity committee may be the preparation of a congregational brochure, or perhaps the planning of a mail campaign. Be sure to tell the truth in all publicity; don't promise more than can be delivered. Rather, identify and highlight the strengths of your church and build on them.

To this point we have looked at attracting the first-time visitor. We will now consider a related question: what attracts the *return* visitor and what is an appropriate and effective strategy with them?

1 Herb Miller, *How to Build A Magnetic Church*, (Nashville: Abingdon Press, 1987) p. 64.
2 Quoted in Miller, *Op Cit*, p. 45.
3 Herb Miller, pp. 45—56.
4 Reported in Research Report: Congregational Tools for Effective Evangelism Project, (The America Lutheran Church, October, 1986) p. 12.
5 Oswald and Leas, p. 54.
6 Baehr, *Getting the Word Out*.

Reflection Questions — Chapter Four

1. Our church is known for its warmth and friendliness. ___ Yes ___ No

2. Our church's worship services are consistently joyful and celebrative. ___ Yes ___ No

3. Our church's worship always echoes with the note of grace. ___ Yes ___ No

4. Our church's worship always enables me to experience the presence of God. ___ Yes ___ No

5. Our church bulletin contains all that is necessary to allow a newcomer to participate fully. ___ Yes ___ No

6. Our church's nursery would get high marks from the most particular of parents.
    ___ Yes ___ No

7. Our church has an outstanding adult education program. ___ Yes ___ No

8. Our church building is in good repair and is neat and appealing. ___ Yes ___ No

9. Our church has ample parking.
    ___ Yes ___ No

10. Our church is pleased to have our pastor spend time in community activities. ___ Yes ___ No

11. Our church has at least one ministry designed to meet needs in the community. ___ Yes ___ No

12. Our church is well known and respected in this community. ___ Yes ___ No

•   In what areas can we improve?

•   What will be our strategy?

•   In the meantime, how can we compensate?

Attracting the Return Visitor

In most churches, second-time visitors receive much less attention than first-time visitors. And third-time visitors may receive little or no attention or intentional response by the church or its people. This is unfortunate, since it has been shown that the receptivity of visitors, and the likelihood of their eventually affiliating with the church, increases dramatically with the second and third visit. Here are three goals to keep in mind as you think about an effective response to your second time visitors:

Goal #1: Identify

If we do not know the person is a visitor, we will not be able to respond to him or her in a personal way. One hopes that a number of people will have learned the person's name as a result of the first visit. As vital as that is, more information is needed, specifically an address which is necessary for follow-up. Again, it may be that the visitor's address has been learned at the time of the first visit. But often first time visitors are reluctant to give their address, or any personal information.

When they return a second time, however, they are indicating that there was something about your church that they liked and they are interested in learning more. Second-time visitors are much more likely to provide an address and telephone number. But what is the best way to obtain this information?

Churches have used a variety of methods with varying results: a guest book in the narthex; visitor's cards in a pew rack or inserted in the bulletin; a visitor's packet with an address card given to visitors who acknowledge their presence by raising a hand; assigning the responsibility to a greeter or usher; and there are others. If your congregation is using one of these methods and it works for you, great. As the saying goes, "If it ain't broke, don't fix it."

However, there is a better method. Before describing it let me say that in the church I served most recently we relied on the guest book method for years. Our greeters asked those persons recognized as visitors to please sign the book. I am sure we had many visitors during those years, but we scarcely averaged one guest signature a month. When we changed methods we discovered that in the next seven years, not a Sunday went by in which we did not have identified visitors. That is why I am partial to this method.

The most effective method of visitor identification, in my view, is the friendship registration pad which is passed down the aisle and signed by each worshipper. That last point is important. It is in large part because everyone signs it that visitors do also. Visitors, as a rule, do not care to be conspicuous, and prefer to do only what everyone does. The friendship register is a pad of pre-printed sheets which contain space for a person's name and address. In addition, a check is made in an appropriate box indicating several choices, such as: member of this fellowship, visitor, "desire a call," etc. Most religious supply houses will have samples on hand.

At an appropriate time in the service, the pastor or worship leader gives a brief verbal welcome and a very brief explanation of the "ritual of friendship" or whatever you choose to call it. Often this is done just prior to receiving the offering, and the pad is passed during the offering. The announcement might be something like this: "In our church we use a friendship register to help us get acquainted. Please write your name on the pad when it reaches you. If you are visiting with us today, we ask that you include your address, so that we can send an acknowledgement of your presence. Thank you."[1]

The effectiveness of this method depends on each person signing. If that does not occur, results will be mixed at best. One other potential weakness in this method is that addresses are requested only of visitors since regular attenders would probably resist writing their address each week, and as a result some visitors will follow their neighbor's example and leave that space blank.   In my experience, that occurs with about ten to twenty percent of first-time visitors, and much less with second-time visitors. Even if you are unable to obtain an address, this method seems best to me. It is minimally disruptive to worship, it does not cause visitors embarrassment or discomfort, and it identifies newcomers more effectively than any other method.

Two additional benefits can come from using friendship registration pads. For one thing, it is an excellent way to monitor the attendance of members. Following worship someone tears off the top sheet of each pad and spends a few minutes sorting the sheets into two stacks. Sheets which include one or more visitor's names are given to the outreach volunteer who records the information for follow-up. The sheets are then returned so that the attendance of all members can be recorded.

The purpose of monitoring members' attendance is not to check up on absent members as if they are skipping church, but rather to enable the congregation to minister effectively to all its constituents. It has been shown that a change in worship attendance is the first indication of a person beginning to drop out of active church involvement. Often, this "back door" can be significantly closed with immediate response and concern shown by the church.[2]

Many times pastors have been unaware that someone in the congregation has been absent. Perhaps there is an illness which is keeping someone away, and the person's absence has not yet been recognized. It may be that a member is beginning to drift away and wonders if he or she will be missed. Recording attendance is the first step to put in place a method of contacting those who are absent — perhaps for two or three weeks in succession — with a friendly phone call. The caller would simply say, "John, we've missed you in church the last few Sundays. I hope there has not been some problem." Most people will be grateful for that kind of call, and the potential dropout rate will almost certainly decline.

A second additional benefit to a church using the friendship register is that it facilitates the process of getting people acquainted. Ordinarily the pads are passed down the row and back so that the pad returns to where it began. This allows each person in the row to note the name of the other persons seated in that row. In large congregations this practice serves an important purpose even when no visitors happen to be seated in the row, since members probably do not all know one another.

Goal #2: Introduce

This is the second important goal in your strategy of welcoming the second or third-time visitor. It is most effectively done by members seated in the same row as the visitor. Encourage members to accept responsibility for the visitors in their row. At the conclusion of the service, members should take the lead in welcoming the visitor, and initiate the conversation which continues as they walk up the aisle.

You can count on the fact that approximately three of every four people are basically shy, and will wait for someone else to begin the conversation. When a visitor is alone in a group of people who are well-acquainted, it is even more unlikely that she or he will take the initiative. But as members are encouraged to introduce themselves to newcomers, a strong positive impression will be left, and the good impression from the first visit will be substantiated.

So what do you say? Often members are reticent about initiating a conversation for fear of quickly running out of things to talk about. Here are some suggestions. Begin by introducing yourself. This is the first, and often the hardest step. Introducing yourself invariably leads to a more extended conversation. Recognize that it is your responsibility to keep the conversation going.

Questions should be kept to a minimum, since they may result in the visitor feeling his or her privacy is being invaded. But one or two questions are proper and necessary. It is always appropriate to ask, "Is this your first visit here?" Should the answer be "yes," you will want to express appreciation for the person's attendance, perhaps making reference to the feelings which might be present on such an occasion. You could identify with the person's feelings of anxiety by commenting on your own first visit to the church.

A second question might be, "What brought you to our church today?" This question can be very helpful in providing information for follow-up. A third question may be appropriate. "Do you live near here?" These are probably the only question you should plan to ask, although of course, other questions might emerge spontaneously from the conversation.

If it becomes apparent that the person is visiting for a second or third time, the conversation could, of course, be different. In either case the goal is to be friendly but not overpowering.

After introductions have been made, the conversation will continue as you are walking up the aisle. When you reach the exit, introduce the visitor to at least one other person. The best approach is to introduce the visitor to a person who is most like the visitor: same sex, approximate age, and similar interests and family status, if possible. If you can match any other characteristics, so much the better. Ideally, the member to whom you have introduced the visitor will now take the lead in dialogue, and in turn, introduce him or her to others. In a relaxed format, that process can continue.

In some congregations, members of the church board are given responsibility for worship visitors. An advantage of this is that board meetings can include talk about the process, with suggestions for procedure and reports of what happened. Board members are assigned certain areas in the sanctuary and asked to minister to any visitor seated in their area. Disadvantages are that the visitor's name will not have been seen (unless the worshipper is in the same row), some visitors will be missed, and initial feelings of discomfort might be experienced by a visitor prior to the board member reaching him or her. This method also appears less natural.

The strategy of using board members might be used as an initial way to get the congregation to adopt the process, or in the case of a congregation where the first method is not working effectively.

Not long ago I was invited to preach in the church I had most recently served as pastor. I wrote an unchurched friend of mine in that city and invited him to attend. He came. (By the way, I continue to be amazed by how many of our unchurched friends will accept a personal invitation to attend a worship service). I very much wanted to speak with Dave after church, but there were many people to greet and a half hour had slipped by before I reached the fellowship area. I assumed my friend had left. To my surprise I saw Dave talking to one of the men in the church. When I greeted him I said, "I didn't know that you knew anyone in this church." Dave replied, "I didn't, but someone came up to me after church to greet me, and introduced me to someone else. After that people just kept introducing me to others and I have not been alone since."

Perhaps that sounds overwhelming, and it may be. But when it occurs naturally and is genuine, it's a powerful demonstration of the church's warmth and friendliness. I know Dave saw it that way, and his experience gave me a wonderful reminder of why I love that church. Here are people sharing Christ's love with strangers, who experience God's love through the love of God's people.

When a visitor is seated near you in worship, introduce yourself and introduce the visitor to someone else. If you are introduced to a visitor, spend some time visiting with the person and then introduce him or her to someone else. When that happens, visitors will feel welcome.

Goal #3: Invite

No visitor (first, second, or third-time) should leave the worship service without having received several invitations from members. Each person who greets and converses with the visitor should plan to invite him or her to something. To begin, the visitor should be invited to a coffee hour.

Coffee/fellowship time after worship is indispensible for the church that intends to attract and keep visitors. It provides an immediate occasion for inviting, and an excellent opportunity for socializing. Without it, visitors are unlikely to remain long enough to meet anyone in the church.

One of the members should extend the invitation and accompany the visitor to the coffee area. Whatever else is offered, there should be a choice of beverages with both hot and cold drinks. After assisting the visitor with refreshment the member continues to visit and introduce the new acquaintance to others.

In some congregations the Christian Education hour follows worship, and an invitation to an appropriate class can be extended. When this occurs the inviter accompanies the visitor to the class and introduces the person to others. Invitations to adult classes and activities are always appropriate. Members will want to describe the group in which they themselves participate and invite the visitor to attend. If the group meets at a time other than immediately following the service, an invitation to the event may also include an offer to stop by and pick up the visitor. Invitations should be specific, as in "Would you care to attend this Thursday?"

Occasionally one will encounter gracious and generous church members who are prepared to offer an immediate invitation for a meal. When our children moved to a distant city, the first time they attended the church of which they are now members, they were invited to someone's home for lunch. One Sunday last year when I visited a church in another city, I was invited to join a group which regularly went out for brunch after church. Even when the visitor's schedule does not allow such an invitation to be accepted, the generosity and grace of the gesture make a powerful impression.

Finally, visitors ought always to be invited to return. One hopes that every member who spends time with the visitor will express appreciation for his or her visit, and invite the person to return. People come back to a church where they feel welcomed, valued, and needed. By contrast, when visitors perceive that no one cares about their presence or desires their return, they will probably not come back.

Why Visitors Return

In developing effective visitor attraction and retention strategy, it is helpful to realize that different factors are at work in attracting the first-time visitor than those which cause the visitor to return. The first-time visitor will generally have come out of some sense of personal need. The needs vary widely, and include such concerns as: the desire for a new beginning for one's life; the need for fellowship with God; a concern to find a place to belong; the wish to affiliate with a new congregation; the hope of finding help with a problem; or perhaps simply a vague yearning for something the person does not have. Whatever the *reason* which brought the first-time visitor — whether it was an advertisement, an invitation, or a program — the *need* was the cause of the person's response. Even in cases where no need could be readily identified by the worshipper, we may take it for granted that a need was present, at least in the sense of some hope, or a feeling of dissatisfaction or incompleteness in life.

The return visitor, by contrast, has come because of the welcome he or she received on the first visit. Worship visitors, says Herb Miller, "base their decision on whether to return by how members act."[3] Only if the first visit has been a positive experience is a second visit likely. It is the warmth and friendliness of the congregation which are the most important factors in making the first visit a positive experience. While the need for a closer fellowship with God, or a place to belong, may still be present in that first-time visitor's life, if the visitor does not experience a warm and caring welcome, she or he will continue their search for fellowship or belonging in another church. The feeling of being welcomed is what brings visitors back.

In addition to the importance of the welcome, first-time visitors need to have the issues addressed which motivated their original visit. To quote Miller again, "If the worship service fails to meet the needs of first-time visitors, no amount of friendliness can convert them to joiners."[4]

If the first visit was a warm and welcoming event, and the person felt it was a beneficial experience, the newcomer will probably return. It may well be that the decision to return is made before the end of the initial visit. If the visitor does return, she or he moves into the stage which is described by Oswald and Leas as "testing."[5] This is a process of evaluating the congregation to see if it is a place where needs can be met in a climate conducive to personal growth and fulfillment. It is a time that involves risking and anxiety.

The testing stage is a tentative exploration: a time of questions and first impressions. During this phase the worshipper is wondering, "Can I find friends here?" "How do I fit in?" "Am I needed and valued?" If, during subsequent visits, the visitor is ignored, the testing process will probably come to an abrupt halt. To not be recognized as a previous visitor can even have a negative effect. The pastor's response to the visitor is particularly important, since the pastor in a sense, personifies the church institution. Equally important is the need to develop a more than superficial relationship with other people in the congregation of similar age, occupation, family status, etc.

Favorable impressions gained in the first few visits help move the visitor from the "testing" stage to the "affiliating" stage. The affiliating stage is like courtship. Oswald and Leas[6] indicate this stage may last from one month to two years. During this period the visitor is no longer shopping around, but settling in to determine whether or not to join.

The questions being explored during this stage include: Is this congregation genuine? Is the pastor the kind of person who can help me? Am I comfortable with the theological views of the congregation? Am I accepted by the members? Let's look at each of these questions...

The issue of genuineness or authenticity was raised earlier. We suggested that, while people seem to have difficulty finding the words to express it, the feeling of reality and genuineness in the worship service and the life of the congregation are important ingredients in what people are looking for. People are looking for "congruence," that is, agreement or harmony between what is heard and what is seen. Does the love and acceptance talked about come through in relationships? Is the Christian life lived out by the members of the congregation? Are these people serious about their faith?

The issue of pastoral effectiveness is very important in the affiliating stage. Most people will not join a church if they do not have respect for and confidence in the pastor. Prospective members focus on the pastor's tasks, especially preaching, teaching, and leading worship. While a level of competence is certainly necessary, I believe that people are less interested in skill than effectiveness. In addition to observing the pastor's performance, the newcomer will be forming opinions about the character and personality of the pastor. Two questions are probably most important: "Does this pastor make faith issues understandable?" and, "Is this pastor a person I feel could help me with a problem?" If these questions are answered positively — and such an opinion tends to be formed fairly quickly — the primary issues concerning the pastor have been addressed in the affiliating stage. Later the newcomers will become more interested in the pastor's relational and leadership skills.

The theological and Biblical stance of the congregation also plays a role as people consider membership. Persons who are already established believers generally choose to join a congregation whose theology is fairly close to their current beliefs. It is increasingly true, however, that more and more people are joining those congregations that are helping people understand the Bible and applying it in a meaningful way to everyday life. People are staying in churches where spiritual needs are met through commitment to biblical truths. Today denominational loyalty is less of a factor in attracting and keeping members than it was in previous generations.

Much has already been written about the need to help newcomers feel accepted. Relationships are of great importance, and the need to feel at home cannot be stressed too much. In the book *Who Cares About Love?* the authors report the results of a survey which indicate that the greater the perceived level of love in a church, the greater its capacity for growth. This is true both for individual congregations and entire denominations. In the survey "it was found that growing churches showed a *significantly* higher love quotient than churches which had declined during the past five years — regardless of denomination. Churches that have learned to love, and to share that love are growing. Churches lacking in love are usually declining. Love, in

Jesus' name, attracts people."[7]   As people feel accepted and valued by members of the congregation, bonding takes place and newcomers begin to feel they belong. When a person feels he or she belongs, the decision to join is natural.

Another item of research is helpful in understanding this issue. In a study on church dropouts, *friendship* emerged as the key ingredient in both bringing people into the congregation and in keeping them active. One hundred people were interviewed, half of whom had joined the congregation and stayed, and half of whom had joined and dropped out. The groups were then compared in terms of the number of friendships each had developed in the church within six months after becoming a member. Here are the results: [8]

Number of New Friends in the Church	0	1	2	3	4	5	6	7	8	9+
Actives	0	0	0	1	2	2	8	13	12	12
Drop-outs	8	13	14	8	4	2	1	0	0	0

Based on this, and additional research, Win Arn suggests, "Each new member should have a minimum of seven new friends in the church within the first six months. Friendship is the strongest bond cementing new members to their new congregation. If new converts/members do not immediately develop meaningful new friendships within their church, expect them to return to their old friends outside the church. Seven new friends are a minimum; ten, fifteen or more are better." [9]

Friendships can begin forming from the first visit by a newcomer. Developing such friendships will play a crucial role in bringing people into the congregation. Two important suggestions: don't assume this happens automatically; and don't wait for it to happen spontaneously. Churches committed to growth intentionally plan means and opportunities for friendships to develop. One important way this occurs is through social events which are part of the church's ministry. Ideally, at least one such event should take place each month. As people come together in social gatherings and have fun together, friendships will be developed and strengthened. Social gatherings provide opportunities for inviting, and inviting, as we have seen, is the single most effective means of bringing new people into the fellowship. Is your congregation an inviting church?

---

1 Herb Miller advises not to use the word "sign" in asking people to record their names, since that word may have a negative effect. Miller, p. 78.

2 For more information on this, see John S. Savage, *The Apathetic and Bored Church Member*, (Pittsford, NY, Lead Consultants, 1976).

3 Miller, *How to Build...*, p. 71.

4 Miller, p. 45.

5 Oswald & Leas, p. 51.

6 Oswald and Leas, pp. 54-58.

7 Win Arn, Carroll Nyquist, and Charles Arn, *Who Cares About Love?*, (Pasadena: Church Growth Press, 1986), p. 119.

8 *Ibid.*, p. 180.

9 *The Church Growth Ratio Book*, p. 23.

Reflection Questions — Chapter Five

Score each answer with a 1, 2, or 3 as follows:

"1" = Not at the present time.
"2" = More or less, but it needs improvement.
"3" = Yes, and it is working effectively.

_____ A. We welcome visitors each Sunday with a printed and verbal welcome.

_____ B. Our members regularly invite non-churched persons to worship.

_____ C. We have an effective method of identifying worship visitors.

_____ D. In our church a visitor would nearly always be greeted by several people.

_____ E. We have a "coffee hour" where members socialize with visitors.

_____ F. Our visitors are introduced to several other people when they attend.

_____ G. Visitors invariably comment about the friendliness of our congregation.

_____ H. People seldom visit our congregation without being invited to return.

_____ I. We have visitors every Sunday.

_____ J. Our congregation always follows-up worship visitors.

From the questions answered with a "2", which would you select for immediate improvement?

From the questions answered "1", which area would you suggest most urgently needs attention?

What can you suggest for addressing these need?

Increasing the Number of Visitors

We have been reminded that the single most effective way to increase worship visitors is through the invitation of church members. As they relate to their friends and relatives, opportunities develop for them to invite these people to worship and to the activities of the congregation. In this chapter we will explore the matter of encouraging invitations from members to prospective new members in more detail. A five-step strategy will be discussed.

STEP ONE Help your members understand and accept responsibility for inviting

In conducting evangelism workshops I often ask, "Who is likely to be more effective in evangelizing ... a well-trained pastor or a typical lay-person?" The answer, of course, is the lay-person. Since that surprises and puzzles some people, we go on to develop reasons why lay-people are more effective. Among the answers usually given are: Lay-people have more contacts with unchurched people; pastors sometimes intimidate;

lay-people more easily identify with other lay-people; lay-people "speak the same language;" and lay-people have more natural opportunities to speak with unchurched persons. These are all significant reasons, but the most important reason has not yet been given. It is this: the invitation of a lay-person has more value than a similar invitation from a pastor.

Consider this: when a pastor invites some-one to church, or speaks positively about the church, that is perceived as part of the pastor's job. The invitation may even be seen as given for the pastor's benefit. The unchurched person may think, "Naturally the pastor would like me to attend his or her church — it will make the pastor look good." The pastor's invitation is thus not always taken at face value. No such disadvantage accom-panies an invitation from a lay-person. The differ-ence between the invitation of a pastor and a lay-person is like the difference in the effect of hearing a new product endorsed by an actor on television and having your neighbor tell you about it.

All believers have a role in evangelism, and lay-people have the leading role. It is vital that we help everyone understand that. Lay-people are best in extending invitations to those outside the church.

STEP TWO Encourage church members to identify people whom they can invite

Research conducted by Church Growth, Inc. reveals that, on the average, a lay-person knows seven to eight people outside the church well enough to have some influence with them.[1] Those are the people most likely to respond to an invitation to church. It is important to encourage laity to identify people in that group, to begin praying regularly for them, to spend time with them, to reach out lovingly in various ways to them, and to invite them to attend worship and/or other events sponsored by the church.

We recognize that friendship and love are offered for their own sake, not as an enticement to allow for evangelizing. We love people because that is what we are called to do by the gospel. In the Church Growth film FOR THE LOVE OF PETE, a moving scene makes the point powerfully. Diane, an active Christian, has been spending time with her friend Judy, who is dealing with the pain of divorce. Judy asks, "Are you being nice to me just so you can convert me?" Diane responds by saying, "My friendship isn't some kind of bait to get you to join my church or become a Christian, but my faith does have something to do with my caring for you." Judy picks up on that right away by blurting out, "I knew there was a catch." Diane assures Judy that her love is given with no strings attached. Judy then raises the critical question: "Will you still be my friend even if I don't want your religion?"

Unless we can give an unequivocal "yes" to that same question, our love is not genuine, and our relationships will not grow strong. If we do love unconditionally, our invitations will be dealt with seriously. It depends to a large degree on our motivation. Are we inviting this person for our sake, or for hers? True evangelism arises from a desire to share what we have experienced with a person we love, in order that that person may also be enriched. We function that way with people we care about. If we read a good book, see a great movie, or discover a delightful new restaurant, invariably we tell someone about it so that they may enjoy it as well. Why should we not do the same with our faith, and our church?

A suggestion which may be helpful is to encourage members of your congregation to identify, and learn to talk about, the value they find in participating in their congregation. Some people write this out in a sentence or two, and call it a brief commercial for their church. The statement might begin with "I love our church because..." or "What I appreciate about our church is..." Such "testimonies" can be introduced into one's conversation at appropriate times, and are very helpful as part of the inviting process.

STEP THREE Provide specific occasions and events for inviting

To do this encourages members of the congregation to break out of the habit of not inviting, and provides excellent opportunities for attracting visitors. While invitations to church are always in order, highlighting definite occasions will be one way to ensure them happening. Here are a few specific events which have been used effectively.

"Special Sundays" This is a term given to designated Sundays on which you encourage members to bring visitors to worship. It is something of a code word, since it allows public announcement of such an event without the need to explain. It can thus be announced in advance, and while members will know what it means (after you have once explained it), visitors will not be aware of its full significance, and thus not be uncomfortable or feel that they are the center of attention.

A special Sunday is a planned occasion for inviting. Usually something out of the ordinary is planned for that worship experience. That is what makes the occasion "special." Perhaps a guest speaker will be present, or a musical group invited to sing. It is the special person or group which provides the occasion for inviting. However, that is not the whole story. On a special Sunday the service is planned with unchurched persons particularly in mind, with everything designed for their circumstances and needs — including the sermon. On these occasions the sermon is always designed to explore faith issues, and to present the gospel clearly and winsomely. The message is prepared to present a case for, and to encourage commitment to, the gospel of Jesus Christ.

When members see an announcement in the church bulletin that September 20 (or whatever) will be a special Sunday in First Church, they should be encouraged to think and pray about whom to invite. They will know that if Harry or Heather attend on that day, they will not hear a sermon on stewardship, but will attend a service completely planned with their circumstances and needs in mind.

Special Sundays can be scheduled about once each quarter. In planning them, use variety. You might have the high school choir sing on one occasion. Perhaps an anniversary or other celebration provides an occasion. Seasons like Christmas and Easter lend themselves beautifully to this emphasis. Some congregations honor and recognize a particular group of people — such as teachers, firemen, little-league coaches, hospital volunteers — on a Special Sunday. Formal and informal invitations are extended to people in that category, and a brief tribute paid them during the worship service. Other ideas for Special Sundays include: Visitors or Friendship Sunday, Open-house Sunday, Grandparents Sunday, Graduates

Day, etc. In some congregations baptisms are the occasion, with printed invitations sent to all the relatives of those who are to be baptized.

In summary, the congregation plans, at least once a quarter, a special service which is announced in advance. Members of the congregation, alerted to this opportunity, identify those whom they will invite to worship on that day. Invariably, a significant number of visitors will attend. I know of two congregations who had nearly as many visitors as regular members at a recent Special Sunday service. A response like that energizes the congregation, and gives added impetus to the congregation's outreach efforts.

"Prospective Member Brunch" This method combines an invitation to worship with an invitation to a post-worship brunch. The brunch can be planned to include both people who have not attended a service and those who are in the testing or affiliating stage. The brunch is designed to include an equal mix of members and non-members.

Begin with two to four people from the congregation to serve as planners. Select a date and place (usually the home of one of the group) for the brunch, and decide how many people will be included. Planners then recruit some people from among those who have most recently joined the church. Enough people are recruited so that, with the original two to four planners, you have gathered a number equal to half the total number planned for the brunch. Each person who helps sponsor the brunch agrees to bring an item of food and a guest.

A brunch planned like this has several advantages. It takes advantage of the unique contribution which can be made by the most recent members of the congregation. Not only are they likely to know more unchurched people than the average church member, but also their own decision is fresh, and with their high commitment and enthusiasm they make outstanding advocates for the church. The relaxed atmosphere of a brunch provides opportunities to socialize, and since there will not be a formal, sit-down meal, it is possible to move around and meet everyone. It is important that the pastor and spouse are invited and given an opportunity to meet people.

If the people being invited to brunch have children, make plans to accommodate them. You might engage a few parents in the church to provide child care, perhaps in one of their nearby homes. Or, teenagers might be engaged to provide child care in the church building during the brunch. The effectiveness of the brunch is greatly enhanced by the provision of responsible child care.

It is important that the invitations be very clearly for worship and brunch. By being honest about that you will avoid appearing manipulative, and having worship included as part of the package creates a link between church attendance and friendship development.

"Social and Recreational Events" We have discussed the importance of providing opportunities for friendships to develop, and suggested it will be helpful to plan a social event each month. Such activities provide ideal opportunities to see visitors develop deeper relationships with members of the congregation. This is increasingly important in our society, since social scientists agree that a desire for person relationships is a characteristic of contemporary life.[2]

Social events should be planned to include prospective members. Members should be encouraged to "bring a friend" whenever groups in the congregation gather informally. For young couples, one effective event is a volleyball party. People bring guests, play every other game, and socialize in between. Snacks at the end of the evening give everyone the chance to visit.

Hospitality and socializing also occur spontaneously in warm and friendly churches. There may well be people in your congregation who will invite newcomers for a meal, perhaps right after worship the first Sunday they attend. This is a wonderful commendation of the church. Others will invite a few people for dinner, and include some recent worship visitors in the mix. You may discover a common interest you share with a newcomer, and invite him or her to be your guest at a concert, boat show, quilting exhibit, or whatever. The important thing is to invite, and to provide specific opportunities for members to invite their friends and new acquaintances.

STEP FOUR Encourage members to invite each other's friends

Dr. Win Arn stresses the importance of newcomers establishing a minimum of seven new friendships during the first 6-12 months of their church affiliation.[3] That begins to happen when members broaden their concerns and interest to include the unchurched friends of other members in the church. When your church friends introduce you to the person they have brought, accept that person as your potential friend as well. Begin planning ways to include such persons in your circle, and invite them to events or to your home.

A congregation in California has developed this principle into a method which is a key part of their outreach strategy. It begins with two couples from the church who make plans to have dinner at couple A's home. Each couple brings an unchurched couple to dinner. The following month, couple B has the group for dinner. By now the four couples are well acquainted. At this second dinner one of the church members asks whether the group would like to meet for an informal Bible study. When this idea is introduced, a few brief provisions are agreed to, such as the number of times they will meet (usually six), the day, place, and time. It will be clear that this will be an informal event with no pressure of any kind.

In the meantime, several other groups have been forming among other churched and un-churched couples. During the third month, three of the groups get together for a cookout at one of the member's homes. Following that, an event is planned each month to which all 24 people are in-vited. Those who participate in these events form deepening friendships, and most of those "new-comers" eventually become part of the church.

As other members build relationships with your unchurched friends, two things begin to happen: 1) your own unchurched friends develop a more accurate understanding of what it means to be a Christian, because they see the variety of ways faith is manifested in people; and 2) you are freed to reach out to, and build relationships with someone else's friend. Such evangelism is very effective in communicating the love of the Christian community to those who are not yet a part of it.

STEP FIVE Build in accountability

Wouldn't it be wonderful if credit were given for good intentions? We'd all be very well off. But in our reflective moments, we recognize that good intentions alone are of no value. How often have you said to yourself, "I ought to invite so-and-so to church, or over for dinner," and yet you haven't? Good intentions (or even good words) cannot make up for failure to act. The apostle John says, "Our love should not be just words and talk; it must be true love, which shows itself in action." (I John 3:18 TEV)

Because we are all prone to make promises to ourselves which are easily broken, we need a system of accountability.[4] A congregation intentional about outreach needs to develop a method by which such mutual support can occur. The best results are seen if it becomes part of the regular agenda of groups and meetings. Lacking that, it will be advisable to provide ways in which members are paired up. The important thing is to provide regular times for mutual support, encouragement, and accountability.

Such meetings should include prayer for one another and for our unchurched friends or family. Planned steps are shared for strengthening rela-tionships with the non-member. Activities can be planned. Suggestions may be offered by those who will be more objective. And, of course, part of the time will include reporting what happened in the intervening weeks. At times someone will need to admit that a planned step was not taken, and that is part of accountability. All this takes place in the context of mutual support, disclosure, and caring.

When this time of sharing and support occurs in the course of a regular meeting (perhaps having the first 20 minutes of the session devoted to this purpose), it serves several important purposes. First, it allows for the over-arching purpose of Christ's church — to make disciples — to be integrated into every function and activity of the church. Second, it provides encouragement for those who may not be experiencing obvious or rapid progress in seeing unchurched friends and family move closer toward the Christian faith. And third, the time of sharing and support will encourage members not presently involved in an evangelistic relationship to take the initiative and try. Building in accountability is an important component of the effective evangelizing process.

Before we leave the subject of inviting, let us return to a subject we raised in a previous chapter. Word of mouth advertising, we said, is by far the most effective kind of advertising. Nothing is as likely to "sell" as the testimony of a satisfied customer. Some people will be uncomfortable with the idea of "selling" the church. Granted, that image can be understood in ways that would be inappropriate. But is it not true that we want to commend the church? To be sure, our ultimate goal is to commend the gospel of Christ, but it is in the church that we both hear and experience that gospel, and we commend the church to those we care about so they may also experience God's love and find their lives transformed by it.

If this is true, we ought not be opposed to the idea of trying to persuade people to attend our church. We do so, not because it is the perfect church, or that other congregations are less worthy, but out of the conviction that in our congregation, where we have experienced God's love and grace, others will experience that grace as well. What we have received from God, including the gift of being part of the community of believers, we wish to share.

If this is so, then let us encourage each other to talk about our congregation. Most of us find it possible to do that, even if we may have difficulty talking about or explaining our faith. We can say what we value and appreciate about our church fellowship. By adding this witness to our invitation, we provide an added reason for people to respond positively. When they come on Sunday morning, we can trust that God will meet them. It is God, after all, who is the true evangelizer.

---

1 *The Master's Plan*, p. 52.

2 *Who Cares About Love?*, p. 34

3 *Church Growth Ratio Book*, p. 23.

4 That is part of the beauty of using THE MASTER'S PLAN KIT. Built into that program is an ongoing way for members of the congregation to encourage and support one another in their efforts to reach out to, and evangelize their friends.

Reflection Questions — Chapter Six

1. Many believe that evangelism is the pastor's job. How would you respond this attitude?

2. If you were invited to give a brief "commercial" for your church, what would you say?

3. When was the last time you invited a friend or relative to attend your church? What happened?

4. Have you ever invited someone to church who said "no"?

   Looking back now, why do you think the invitation was declined?

   From your present perspective, can you think of anything you might have done differently?

   Can you think of a way you might invite that person again, now?

5. What is the first name of the person you are presently seeking to evangelize?

   How frequently is that person in your prayers?

   What specific acts of kindness have you done for that person recently?

   Have you spent time with that person recently?

   Have you spoken of your faith with that person?

   Do you feel ready to invite that person to attend church with you? Can you say why?

6. Have you met a non-churched person at a church event who was brought by someone else? How could you reach out to that person?

7. How does your church encourage members in evangelizing, and hold each other accountable?

Helping Visitors Become Members

The process of evangelization is not complete until those who have responded to the claims of Christ are active, functioning members of a local Christian church. In other words, the goal in evangelism is not to get "decisions," but to make "disciples." Even when a person can identify the exact moment of his or her conversion, it would be a mistake to assume that the process of evangelism was completed at that time. "Evangelization" is a preferred word because it indicates that God is working through an on-going process.

Our Lord's Great Commission provides both the authority for this process and its scope: "Go therefore and make disciples of all nations" (Matthew 28:19). David Watson observes that "The verb *to disciple* describes the process by which we encourage another person to be ... a follower of Jesus; it means the methods we use to help that person to become mature in Christ and so be in a position where he or she can now disciple someone else."[1] The goals of evangelization, and a congregation's plan of outreach, should include:

1. enabling a person to make a commitment to Jesus Christ;
2. facilitating a person's entrance and participation in a community of faith;
3. encouraging commitment to a congregation through membership;
4. enhancing a person's involvement in the life of the congregation through worship, nurture, and service; and
5. assisting in a person's life of obedience and discipleship in the world.

Much of our attention in the previous chapters has been on what we have identified as the second step in this process — facilitating a person's entrance and participation in a community of faith. We have focused on this issue for three reasons. First, for a majority of people who become disciples, that is the first step taken. By that we are suggesting that most people are brought to faith through the life and ministry of a local church. A majority of adult Christians grew up in the church and were called to faith and commitment through the church in which they were nurtured. Other people, who became Christians as adults, will also have been called to faith by the ministry of a local church. Their first exposure to that community might have been through a social affair, a class or a group that meets in the church. More probably, it began with attendance at worship. In any event, it was through the life and ministry of the church that they heard the call to faith and responded to it.

A second reason for focusing on congregational outreach is that every Christian, no matter what his or her gifts, can participate in this part of the evangelization process. By that we mean that as the church carries out a variety of ministries; as it offers a variety of invitations; and as it encourages involvement in a variety of tasks, each person in the congregation can find a place where his or her gift may be used in the congregation's ministry of evangelization.

Third, reaching the goal of facilitating a person's entrance and participation in the local church provides the greatest probability that the other goals of the evangelization process will also be reached. If we are able to encourage people to participate in the life of the church, we may expect that they will become maturing disciples, since they will be shaped by the Word of God and supported and encouraged by the people of God.

In this and the following chapter, we will consider the other goals identified as part of the evangelization process. While our primary concern will be with the third and fourth goals, we will also have something to say about the other two goals.

Let's begin with the first goal — enabling a person to make a faith commitment to Jesus Christ. How do you understand this step to take place in your congregation's ministry?

At least three answers can be identified among churches with which I am familiar. Each approach has its strengths and weaknesses. As with much else in a church's ministry of outreach, it is less important to argue for the superiority of one plan than it is to have a definite plan, and to be involved in the on-going tasks of implementing and evaluating the plan. Your congregation's leadership team will surely want to be clear about the question of how people who begin to associate with the church are encouraged to make a commitment to Christ.

In some congregations, the matter is dealt with through the regular preaching and teaching ministry. Some type of invitation is given, which might range from questions in a sermon, to an opportunity to meet with the pastor, to a regular altar call. The assumption is that God calls through the Word, and the church's ministry involves issuing that call to those who come in contact with the church, thus enabling a response of faith and commitment.

A second way to deal with the issue of extending an invitation to Christian faith is through the new members class, or a pre-membership class. Ordinarily, when this strategy is adopted, such a class is a requirement for all of those desiring membership in the congregation. The class may well be designed for persons who are considering membership as well. The members of the congregation are encouraged to invite worship visitors to attend the class, and various other invitations may be used to stimulate attendance. A presentation of the gospel takes place in the class, and participants are challenged with the claims of Christ.

A third method is to deal with the presentation of the gospel through evangelistic visitation. Ordinarily, some members of the church will have been trained in presenting the gospel and inviting a response. A number of models exist. Many congregations, however, successfully develop their own training program for such evangelistic visitation. Generally, when this method is employed, those who have been visiting the church will, at some point, be visited by evangelistic callers, who will go through some type of presentation of the gospel and offer an opportunity for response. This might be the focus of an initial visit to an unchurched person, but it is better if it is not. In my view, it is desirable to have at least one friendly visit prior to any evangelistic call.

The question which needs to be answered is this: "Are you, and the members of your congregation, clear about the way in which you expect the visitors to your church to hear the call to discipleship?"

We have suggested five goals in the evangelizing process. Two of those we have now dealt with — the challenge of calling persons to make a commitment to Jesus Christ, and facilitating the entrance of people into the community of faith. The remainder of this chapter will be devoted to the third goal — encouraging commitment by visitors to the congregation through membership.

Visitor Follow-Up

The first task to be addressed in the process of helping visitors become members is to develop and implement a plan for visitor follow-up. Three principles of visitor follow-up apply to every church: first, it is a deep necessity. Without visitor follow-up, we ignore the single most promising source of potential new members. Second, follow-up of visitors needs to be prompt. And third, lay members of the church should make the initial contact.

Herb Miller reports fascinating statistics on these last two issues. (Miller, in fact, advocates home calls on visitors immediately after their initial attendance at worship, which we will discuss in a moment.) He writes: "When lay-persons make fifteen-minute visits to the homes of first time worship visitors within thirty-six hours, 85 percent of them return the following week. Make this home visit within seventy-two hours, and 60 percent will return. Make it seven days later, and 15 percent will return. The pastor making this call, rather than lay-persons, cuts each result in half."[2] If Miller is right, one can scarcely avoid the conclusion that prompt visits by lay people are of great significance.

While these principles of visitor follow-up are universal to all churches, the methods of visitor follow-up are not. What is the "best" method? That question can only be answered on an individual basis. However, it is helpful to explore the methods of follow-up by considering several questions:

1.   What are various methods used in follow-up?

Personal letter. A letter from the pastor is sent on the day following the first visit from a non-member. The letter expresses thanks for the visitor's attendance, may say something about the congregation's identity and program, and invites the visitor to return. It should be personally addressed and salutated, and signed personally by the pastor. If the pastor adds a phrase or two as a postscript written with a pen, that personal touch will increase the letter's effectiveness. So will a hand addressed envelope. A brochure from the church is an appropriate inclusion.

Telephone call. This is a brief "thank you for coming call," made by a lay member in the congregation. As suggested, it will be most effective if made within thirty-six hours of the visitor's attendance at worship, and may be in response to the first and/or second visit. In addition to thanking the person for coming, and inviting him or her to return, the caller should also mention something which he or she particularly values about the church.

<u>Visit</u>. A visit in the home is the most important and effective aspect of visitor follow-up. Let's look at it more closely.

2. When should a home visit take place?

Home visits should take place immediately after a non-member attends worship the first time. Researchers in church growth testify that this practice produces the best results. I must confess, however, that I am uncomfortable with this. In my view, a call after a first-time visit is a bit too high powered, and might cause a person to feel pressured. Personally, I prefer to delay a home call until the visitor has attended worship at least twice, and to have the phone call and/or letter take place after the initial visit.

3. What is the approach used in a home visit?

The visit should be made by lay-people, generally in teams of two. To call with a partner provides support and security. Lay-people used in the calling program will be selected on the basis of relational skills, and will go through a training process.[3] The number of callers needed can be determined by calculating the average number of home visits to be made in a typical month and recruiting half of that number of people to serve as the calling team.

In recruiting for the calling team, here are some suggestions: people are asked to serve for one year. They agree to attend an initial training session, to meet for one hour each month, and to make at least two calls per month. The training session deals with how-to-do-it issues, and the monthly meeting is for reporting, evaluation, prayer, and assignments. In some congregations, certain members of the calling team receive additional training in personal evangelism and are used in evangelistic calling.

The purpose of follow-up calls is primarily to demonstrate and develop friendship. While the friendliness and warmth of the congregation will hopefully have been experienced at worship, a visit in the home reinforces these feelings and creates a sense of being cared about. Miller identifies five goals for a home visit: (1) to get acquainted, (2) to answer any questions they have about your church, (3) to learn about their religious background and needs, (4) to leave them a brochure describing your church, and (5) to invite them back.[4]

4. Should a church use the telephone in advance or simply drop-in?

Many argue passionately for the unan-nounced, drop-in approach. The contention is that in the overwhelming majority of cases people making drop-in calls are received graciously. Yet I can only say that I do not personally care for this method and would not use it. Why not do the cour-teous thing and call first to see if such a visit is ap-propriate? Of the calling programs in which I have been personally involved, we found that by following this approach we saved time, created positive good will, and were very rarely turned down.

If you are using the telephone approach, the call should be made on Sunday afternoon of the day the visitor attended your church. The caller, after identifying himself, indicates a desire to make a brief visit on behalf of the church, and asks the visitor if it would be convenient to stop by for about fifteen minutes at 7:30 that evening (or perhaps Monday evening). If a scheduling conflict arises, another time can usually be arranged. Most of those who have visited your church, and virtually all who have visited more than once, will be glad to arrange such a visit. If they are not, they probably are not ready to take a step toward membership.

Assignments for calls can be made on a rotation basis by a lay volunteer who functions as a home visit coordinator. Ideally, the church will have developed a system which allows calls to be assigned immediately after worship. In most cases it should be possible to hand an assignment card to a member of the calling team before the person has left the church building. Ray Sells, designer of "The Caring System," recommends that the home visit coordinator make every effort to match similar characteristics (age, marital status, family status, occupation, etc.) of the visitor and the church member/s assigned to follow up. [5]

Suggestions for Making the Visit

More specific guidelines for making a home visit should be included in the training session. But here is a list of some things to do and to avoid.

Don't...

1. Carry a Bible and/or visible material. To do so may intimidate.
2. Apologize for your visit.
3. Ask too many personal questions.
4. Argue, or attempt to refute anything said.
5. Criticize another church/pastor, or listen to such criticism. Instead, change the subject.
6. Push for a response.

Do...

1. Pray before you make the call.
2. Sit where you can face everyone, if possible.
3. Decide in advance who will begin the conversation, and seek to share in it equally.
4. Keep the visit focused on the people being visited, and listen reflectively.
5. Be sincere, genuine, and natural.
6. Affirm your church in specific ways.
7. Be sensitive to appropriate ways to express your faith.
8. Thank them for allowing the visit.
9. Ask permission to pray, and offer a brief prayer of thanks for the visit, as well as for the family or person being visited.
10. Leave gracefully, don't linger or say why you are leaving.
11. Promptly write down notes you need to make, but not while parked in front of their house.
12. Look for them in church. Greet them and introduce them to someone else.

In some calls the person being visited may say something which seems to sidetrack or derail the conversation. Often one is not sure about the issue which is behind such a remark. In such cases, a facilitating response may help the caller understand and deal with the underlying cause. Some examples of such remarks and possible responses follow:

1. The person indicates he or she is not planning to join your church. *Response:* "I hope nothing made you uncomfortable when you visited."

2. The person asks a question you cannot answer. *Response:* "That is a good question. I don't know the answer, but I would like to try to find out and talk about it with you later."

3. The person finds fault with something in your church. *Response:* "Thank you for telling us about that. Perhaps you might have an idea of what could be done about it."

In each case, you have several purposes. You would like to gain more understanding of the issue so that you can respond appropriately. You want to avoid conflict and manipulation. You want the person to feel comfortable and unpressured. You also wish to achieve the purpose of your visit and leave the person feeling that he or she has been understood and accepted. Facilitating comments which encourage further conversation about the subject are ideal in such situations.

One further matter in connection with making home visits is the issue of asking questions. Something of a dilemma is present in this regard, since questions can be both a wonderful means of opening conversations to a deeper level, and a means of closing them. If questions are asked which create discomfort, they are counter-productive and prevent the conversation from going much further.

It is not possible to offer guidelines which indicate when questions will have a positive effect, and when questions will have a negative effect. A few observations, though, can be made. First, in the initial stages of a relationship, and especially in an initial conversation, questions should be used sparingly. Generally, the less familiar we are with a person, the greater should be our caution in asking personal questions. Second, when asking questions, it is wise to ask them in such a way that the person is not forced to respond to a question. Third, one needs to be sensitive to the emotional climate of the conversation in determining whether a question is appropriate. Finally, if a question is asked which produces discomfort, or results in silence, the person who asked the question should move the conversation in a different direction.

We have been suggested that in an initial call on a visitor the primary purpose is the development of friendship. However, members of the church's calling team should be trained to look for natural conversational opportunities to bear witness to their experience with God. Such comments may give rise to responses which indicate the openness of the person to pursue this matter. That provides an opportunity to move to an exploration of spiritual issues. It will be wise to look for ways to encourage further conversation and to recognize the possibility that the person is ready to make a faith commitment. All callers should be prepared to respond appropriately whenever this occurs.

Developing and Using A Responsibility List

For effective follow-up that sees prospective members become actual members, your congregation should maintain an up-to-date file of the names of people you are seeking to reach. Each name may be placed on a 3 x 5 card, along with address, phone number, history of involvement with the church, and information about contacts which have been made with the person. The cards are placed in a file alphabetically, and updated with each subsequent contact.[6]

Names may be gathered from two sources. One involves asking members of the congregation to submit names of persons known to be unchurched. A planning committee then determines an appropriate way for contacting these people. In some churches, members make personal calls on those whose names have been submitted. Another method of contact is a letter indicating that you are sending information about your church and its ministry, and you plan to send them periodic mailings for a limited period. Such a letter may suggest that if they do not wish to be included, they may call to have their names removed. With this "mail campaign" you plan perhaps six mailings over a one-year period. The key issue is to determine what to include in each mailing.[7]

A second source of names for your responsibility list are those of people who have had contact with your congregation. That would include parents whose children attend your church school or other activity, people who participate in a program sponsored by your church, recent worship visitors, and others who have had contact with your ministry. Generally, such people will be put on your mailing list as "friends of the church." Periodically, a special mailing will be sent to these folks. For example, a personal letter of invitation to attend an "Inquirer's Class" (or whatever you call it) can be sent whenever such a class is about to begin.

Regardless of how you acquire the names for your responsibility list, the next important step is to initiate a contact with these persons, by a member of your calling team. When a call is assigned the caller is given information about the person or family, and agrees to a prompt contact. While there is no one "right" approach, here is a typical method: a phone call is made in which the caller introduces him or herself as a member of such and such church, refers to the link between the person and the church which resulted in the call, and indicates that some people in the congregation are planning to stop in to briefly visit some friends of the church. The caller then asks if the person would have about 15 minutes Tuesday at around 8 p.m. If the person indicates a conflict, the caller says, "The following week we could come on Thursday evening, if you have any time available then."

Suppose once again the person indicates a conflict. The caller then asks if there would be a convenient time in the near future. If no positive response is forthcoming, the caller says something like this: "Mrs. Jones, it sounds as if you are not particularly interested in a visit from the church just now." Should Mrs. Jones acknowledge that, the caller would briefly communicate the church's interest in and concern for this person; and give an open invitation by the church to be available at any time of need.

After the telephone call is concluded, the result is noted on the card and signed and dated by the person who telephoned. The card is then returned to the church office, and added to the "non-receptive" file. Each card is reviewed for possible appropriate contact every six months. Four times then, over a two year period, the person is contacted by the church. If no interest has been shown during this period, the fourth phone call should be the final call until some other event indicates an additional contact would be appropriate.

When a telephone contact results in a scheduled appointment, the caller plans a 15 minute friendly visit in which the purpose is to express interest, offer friendship, and invite participation. The church member should focus on the value he or she receives from involvement in the church and leave an attractive brochure which has been prepared for this purpose.

How People Are Brought Into A Church

A helpful study on how people gain entry into a congregation has been written by Arlin Routhauge, an Episcopal priest. He points out that "the most effective means of carrying out a new member ministry varies with the size of the congregation." [8] Routhauge divided congregations into four groups according to the number of active members who attend worship with some regularity. Each group was given an identifying name:

Small church: up to 50 active members; a family church.
Medium size church: 50-150 active members; a pastoral church.
Large church: 150-350 active members; a program church
Extra-large church: 350 and above; a corporation church

The words Routhauge uses to describe churches in each category are both descriptive images for the nature of each size congregation and a clue to the appropriate strategies for new member incorporation.

A similar treatment of size related to member incorporation strategy is presented in *The*

First Year, a book published by the United
Methodist Church. Entry issues are identified for
small, medium, and large size churches.[9] The
author uses "average worship attendance" as the
determiner of congregational size, and suggests
that "small" churches are those averaging up to 50
in worship, "medium" includes congregations
averaging 50 to 175 in worship, and "large"
churches are those averaging more than 175 in
worship.

Reading both of these sources will be
beneficial, since each makes important
contributions. For my own experience, I have
found it practical to consider three size groups;
small, medium, and large, and assume that
"large" churches are those which average above 150
in worship. Let's consider each of these three
groups and examine some strategies for extending
a sense of welcome and belonging.

The Small Church . . . The Family Church

The image of the small membership church
is that of family, and the process by which
newcomers enter is adoption. The crucial need for
the new member incorporation process into such a
church is for a "matriarch" or "patriarch" who
will perform that task. This must be a key lay
leader with influence. That person reaches out to
the newcomer with friendship, and also serves as
the welcomer whose active acceptance of the
newcomer encourages others to receive him or her
into the family.

In addition to being adopted into the small
church family, the congregation must provide four
additional items for the newcomer to be effectively
incorporated:

1. Knowledge of the history and tradition of the congregation.

Small membership churches are often tied strongly to their past. Newcomers will become part of the family by learning — and identifying with — the story of the life and history of the family. We can see that even in the Old Testament. This process of passing on the heritage occurred: "When your son (or daughter) asks you in time to come, 'What is the meaning of the testimonies and the statutes and the ordinances which the Lord our God has commanded you?' then you shall say to your son, 'We were Pharaoh's slaves in Egypt; and the Lord brought us out of Egypt with a mighty hand'...." (Deuteronomy 6:20, 21). Notice how history is related, and that the teller and the hearer are incorporated as one. The history of the past reaches into the future to bring the newcomer into the family. This is of major importance in bringing people into the church today, particularly into "family" churches.

2. A "sponsor" or mentor.

In addition to the "matriarch" or "patriarch," a newcomer needs someone from whom more information about the church can be gained on a continuing basis. Since the patriarch will be one of the congregation's primary leaders, one cannot assume that this person will continue to provide the ongoing information about relationships, roles in the church, customs, etc., which will be needed if the newcomer is to fully belong. In some congregations, a sponsor is formally assigned to be with and to support a new member for the first year of membership.

3. Contact with the congregation's leadership.

   To be personally known by the key church leaders facilitates the process of bonding. It also allows one's personality and gifts to be recognized and used in the life of the church. Both newcomer and congregation thus benefit from regular and planned contact between the congregation's leaders and those who are uniting with the church.

4. Socializing with members, particularly in the homes of members.

   Fellowship, particularly that which involves sharing a meal, has long been recognized as a key to developing deeper relationships. Being invited to someone's home is an invitation to friendship. Since small membership churches sometimes feel "closed" to outsiders, invitations from active members to new-comers for a meal in their home is an important step in the process of bringing them into the family. Suggested approaches for new member incorporation in the small church:

   a) Identify those persons who can fill the roles of "patriarchs" and those who can serve as mentors, and encourage their involvement.

   b) Set up informal meetings, perhaps over a meal, with leaders and all the new members.

   c) Encourage the pastor to offer personal friendship and support. It may be the pastor who takes the role of sponsor.

   d) Involve relatives and friends of the new-comer in the incorporation process. Help them understand the key role they play in assisting the newcomer to become part of the family and in learning about the life of the church.

The Medium Size Church ... The Pastoral Church

Whereas in the smaller membership church, the pastor's role as leader is often less important, in the medium size church, the pastor's leadership is crucial. In fact, the pastor is not only the glue which holds the congregation together, but also the key for new members to become incorporated into the life of the church.

The pastor's role is key because in the more complex medium size church there are usually several family groups and more than one ministry program at the heart of the church's life. It is thus the pastor who provides a common purpose and identity for the various groups and functions that will play a part in welcoming and involving the newcomer. When the pastor is an effective leader, it will be the pastor to whom the congregation looks for direction, inspiration, and ideas. A pastoral church is one in which the pastor is the key person in facilitating effective interpersonal ministry.

Within this context, the new member must experience at least three things before he or she becomes fully incorporated into the medium size church.

1. Personal attention from and nurturing by the pastor.

This is the primary need, and it involves recognition and support of the newcomer. A personal visit in the newcomer's home by the pastor, early in his or her involvement with the congregation is extremely helpful. In addition, the pastor should introduce the newcomer to other members, thus lending support (almost permission) for the entry process.

2. Friendship with a minimum of seven other members.

A doctoral study comparing active church members with inactive dropouts found that active members made an average of seven new church friends in the first six months of membership, in contrast to the dropouts who made only two. [10]

While newcomers do not need to know everyone, "loving attention by a few lay people tells the new members that the congregation's claim to be a caring fellowship is not an empty one, and that there may indeed be places for them within the fellowship."[11]

3. Points of entry.

Leaders must provide "doors" through which newcomers become active members. An entry point or a door is a program in the church which provides a place where newcomers can participate and contribute, as well as make friends in this smaller group setting. Typical points of entry in a medium size church might include: an adult study group, a choir, or a service project.

Suggested approaches for new member incorporation in the medium size church:

a) The pastor should make a call on every third time visitor. (This assumes a previous call has been made by a lay member.)

b) Identify people in the congregation with good hospitality skills. These are people who remember names, exude a feeling of warmth, and carry on conversations with relative ease. Assign several such persons each Sunday morning to arrive early, stay late, and initiate relationships with newcomers.

c) Challenge each group and organization in the congregation to have a plan, and a person, responsible for welcoming visitors and newcomers. Consider methods of encouraging attendance by newcomers, and ways to help them become incorporated into the group.

The Large Member Church ...
The Program Church

In the large membership church the program is the key to the new member's entry and belonging. In a congregation of this size it is no longer possible for the pastor (at least the senior pastor) to play the primary role in the incorporation process of newcomers. Routhauge makes the point that the larger the congregation, the more important it is to have an organized system of new-member incorporation. In most congregations of this size it is advisable to have an incorporation committee to monitor this process.

An effective approach to new member incorporation in the larger church will involve acquainting the newcomer with the people and programs of the church. This means a "new member orientation" program that would include the provision of a membership directory, preferably with pictures, and also indexed by special interests, spiritual gifts, family and/or marital status, occupation, and other areas that help define the person.

The new member orientation system should also introduce the person to the congregation's statement of purpose, a list of program opportunities and locations, a list of officers and structures and other pertinent information about the life and ministry of the local church.

A planned program of new member incorporation should also include and monitor:

- An orientation session or class before joining;
- Regular contacts by letter, phone, home visits;
- Provision of friendship and support, especially during the first year of membership;
- Encouragement to participate in a group;
- Assistance in finding a place to serve;
- A method for monitoring church, Sunday School, and small group involvement;
- A clear understanding of who is responsible for each part of this process.

Suggested approaches for new member incorporation into the larger church:

a) Appoint a task force to evaluate the effectiveness of present methods of incorporation and suggest improvements.

b) Prepare a new member packet of materials to be distributed to those in the entry process.

c) Plan a way to recognize and honor members on the first anniversary of their membership.

d) Develop a strategy to bring new members into the group making calls on newcomers.

As a leader in your congregation, you will want to help your church to develop, practice, and evaluate an intentional process for the incorporation of all new members.

1 David Watson, *Discipleship* (London: Hodder and Stoughton, 1981) p. 66.

2 Miller, pp. 72, 73.

3 A helpful new training course for visitation teams is available from Church Growth, Inc. 2670 S. Myrtle, Monrovia, CA 91016, entitled NIGHT OF CARING.

4 Ibid, p. 76.

5 The Caring System, p. 17

6 "The Caring System" is one pre—packaged approach which can help you organize such a prospect follow—up system. It is available from Church Growth, Inc. 2670 So. Myrtle, Monrovia, CA 91016.

7 See pages 48 and 49.

8 Arlin J. Routhauge, *Sizing Up A Congregation* (New York, NY: The Episcopal Church Center, n.d.).

9 Suzanne Braden, *The First Year*, (Nashville: Discipleship Resources, 1987), pp. 9-32.

10 Flavil Yeakley "Persuasion in Religious Conversion" University of Illinois, 1975. Summarized in Yeakley, *Why Churches Grow* (Arvada, CO: Christian Communications Inc., 1979), p. 54.

11 Braden, op. cit. p. 19.

Reflection Questions — Chapter Seven

1. What is the reason for preferring the term "evangelization" to that of evangelism?

2. Do you agree with the suggestion of the five goals of evangelization? Why or why not?

3. What plan does your congregation follow in encouraging faith commitments to Jesus Christ?

4. What method does your congregation employ for visitor follow-up? How many lay people are involved?

5. When and how do you think home visits should be made with those who have attended your worship service?

6. How would you respond if it became clear that someone you were talking with was ready to make a commitment to Christ?

7. Does your congregation have and regularly work with a responsibility list?

8. What do you understand about how people are brought into the church?

9. What strategy for this is employed in your church?

10. One new thing I learned in this chapter is:

From New Member
To Active Member

We all know, only too well, the seriousness of the drop-out problem. Ezra Earl Jones, General Secretary of the Board of Discipleship in the United Methodist Church, points out in a forward to Braden's book, that within the first year "over fifty percent of new members choose to fade from a commitment to their congregation."[1] The single most effective way to counteract that unfortunate situation is to correct it at the beginning, by doing the best we can with the incorporation process.

A mistake easily made is to assume that once the new member has formally joined, the task of welcoming is complete. That is simply not true. The process goes on.

Understanding Incorporation

Three terms are often used to describe the process by which a person moves from new membership to active membership: "assimilation," "integration," and "incorporation." All three

words communicate the important theme of welcoming the new member into the family:

"Assimilation" — to absorb into the tradition of
a group.
"Integration" — to coordinate or blend into a
unified whole.
"Incorporation" — to unite in or as one body; to
admit to membership into a corporate body.

The term "incorporation" seems preferable,
because it includes the idea of "body," which is the
best image for the church, and because it includes
both the thought of entrance into and unity with the
body. We will use this term in this chapter. [2]
One important assumption about the new
member incorporation process is that the local
church is primarily responsible for helping
newcomers become active, incorporated members.
It is wise to think about the issue in this way
because it helps us realize that when a recent
member becomes inactive, it is usually because of a
failure of the congregation. By recognizing and
identifying specific tasks of the congregation in this
incorporation process, it is possible to evaluate the
ministry needed at various stages in the process.
Three primary needs must be met if
newcomers are to truly and fully belong. They must
develop *friendships* within the church. If a
number of people join the church at the same time,
and have gone through a membership class
together, friendships will already have formed.
Additional friendships with long-time members are
also important. Without friendships within the
congregation, most new members will not stay.
The second need is for the newcomer to
become part of a *group* within the church. Since it
will not be possible to know and be known by

everyone in the congregation, a small fellowship group experience is of great importance. It is here that the caring of the congregation becomes personally experienced. Since groups tend to become more and more difficult to enter as they continue their life, many congregations try to begin new groups on a regular basis. If the new members class has ten or more people, it might continue as an on-going group after membership has taken place. At that point a deeper study of the church's beliefs would be richly rewarding.

The third need for a newcomer is to find a meaningful *task* or *role* to fill. When that happens, the person is giving as well as receiving, and an important goal of discipleship has been reached. If the people who join your congregation have found friends, a group, and a task in the church, they are well on their way to being fully incorporated.

W. Charles Arn, vice-president of Church Growth, Inc., has identified eight characteristics of an incorporated member. According to Arn, these characteristics should be observable in new members by the time the new members class has concluded:

1. Each new member should be able to list at least seven new friends they have made in the church.
2. Each new member should be able to identify his or her spiritual gift/s.
3. Each new member should be involved in at least one (preferably several) roles, tasks, ministries in the church, appropriate to their spiritual gift.
4. Each new member should be actively involved in a small fellowship (face-to-face) group.

5. Each new member should be demonstrating a regular financial commitment to the church.
6. Each new member should personally understand and identify with the goals of the church.
7. Each new member should be exhibiting a regular pattern of worship attendance.
8. Each new member should have identified his/her unchurched friends and relatives and be taking specific steps to help them toward responsible church membership.[3]

If a strategy for seeing each of these goals realized has been identified, you are well on the way to seeing new members become fully incorporated and joyfully contributing members.

The New Member Class

The new member class plays a vital role in the process of incorporating people into the life of the church. A number of different terms have been used to describe such a class. Among those with which I am familiar are "new members class," "pastor's class," "inquirers class" and "orientation class." Clearly, the purpose of such a class will help in the selection of the title. Ordinarily, an orientation class is taught for persons who have already become members and are being helped to understand the church which they have joined. Some of the agenda for such a class will be dealt with in the next section. A pastor's class may be either for persons who are considering joining, or for those who are in the joining process. A new members class is for people who have made the decision to join and who are being helped in the process. An inquirers class is for people who are considering membership.

In spite of those clear differences in meaning, in reality any class is likely to include both persons who have decided to join and those who are exploring the issue. In fact, probably all such classes ought to intentionally include both groups. This chapter is being written with the assumption that the new members class does include both of the groups.

Let's think about people who are exploring membership. If they are to be included in a class, or if a class is to be held for them, it will need to be made clear that they will not be pressured, and that no one will try to persuade them to join the church. Their invitation will be to explore the meaning and significance of membership in the church. Automatic movement into membership should never be assumed since membership involves a personal decision which can only be made on the basis of individual faith.

If a class includes people who are exploring membership, one thing it clearly needs to deal with is the meaning of discipleship. How does one become a Christian? What does it mean to believe and to belong? Part of the agenda in such a class will be to look at the central message of the gospel and to present God's plan of salvation. Further, to do this in such a way that people clearly hear the call of Christ, understand the implications of their response, and in freedom, are allowed to answer.

Many of the people who are in a new members class will have already made such a decision and will be ready to learn about the significance of joining this congregation. We now turn our attention to questions that are raised about the new members class.

Do we need a new members class?

Often, when this question is asked it reflects the situation in a small member church where a class seems unnecessary, or in a congregation not experiencing growth where a class seems impossible. The unspoken assumption behind such a question is that few people are likely to attend. But while the style and format of a new member class in a small membership congregation would differ from that in a larger church, it is quite possible to have an effective class with two to four people. Even if just one new person is joining, a "class" can be formed with the new member and someone from the congregation who functions as sponsor. Orientation always needs to take place, in any size congregation, and issues of entry and belonging are at least as significant in small churches as in large. In fact, the smaller the congregation, the more difficult entry may be. All congregations need a new members class.

Who should attend the class?

In most congregations the people expected to join a new members class can be divided into four groups. They include people who are already church members and are transferring their membership to a new congregation; people who are making their initial commitment to Christ and the church; people who are returning to the church and renewing their commitment after a period of inactivity; and children who have grown up in the church and are now becoming full members.

Should people in all four of these groups attend a new members class? If so, should they all attend the same class? My response to the first question is a definite "yes." I lean increasingly to the view that the new member's class should be a requirement for membership. High demand enhances the importance of this step people are taking, and makes membership significant. All those joining the church, no matter what their age, background, or circumstances, should understand the meaning and implications of this step being taken. Many congregations, in fact, have adopted the policy that a prospective member cannot miss more than two sessions of the class in order to be considered for membership. I think this is a good plan.

Should all groups considering membership be included in the same class? That question is more difficult. Most churches would be ready to include all adults, but what about the children coming into membership? Much depends upon what age they will be, but probably circumstances and needs are sufficiently different that separate classes ought to be held for them where that is possible. The tradition of holding "confirmation" classes already exists in many churches and provides a natural opportunity to deal with membership issues. I believe it most important that the teacher of such a class make clear that class participants do not automatically "graduate" to membership, and encourage a conscious, voluntary decision by those who will be affirming their faith through membership.

How often should new member classes be held?

The first six months of a new member's life in the church are critical. By the end of the sixth month, the new member has probably made up his or her mind whether this church is a place to call home. Therefore, a class scheduled only once a year is not sufficient. In considering timing, it is advisable to take advantage of natural church interest and activity during the year, such as early fall, Advent and Christmas, Lent and Easter. Plan a class schedule which allows invitations to be extended to people who may begin attending the church during these seasons.

It is ideal to plan and announce a year's schedule of new member classes. Unfortunately, many congregations hold new members classes only when enough potential participants can be identified to warrant scheduling. This passive approach is "reactive" rather than "active" and may be a characteristic in other areas of church life, which then becomes a "self-fulfilling" prophecy. The result of a planned and publicized schedule is a sense of expectancy ... "we are going to receive new members." Pastors and other leaders are motivated to play an active role in encouraging attendance at the class. Prayers have a specific focus.

Not all congregations will choose to adopt the same schedule. In my opinion a minimum of at least two new members classes per year should be planned, one in the spring and one in the fall. One would think every congregation can manage that. Most are capable of offering three sessions, scheduled in fall, winter, and spring, which is a good standard for most congregations. In churches which attract many visitors, new member classes may be scheduled back to back or even overlap throughout the year.

How many sessions should be scheduled?

In my experience the most common answer is "six." However, an increasing number of congregations are moving to twelve sessions. I support this decision. It allows much more ground to be covered and is much better for integrating members into the mainstream of church life. A model which I personally like is to schedule the class on a week night for two hours. The first fifty minutes is spent in a formal presentation of content. Following that is a twenty minute break with refreshments, and the last fifty minutes involves small group discussion on a specific topic for the evening. The pastor will generally lead the first part of the session. The discussion time may be led by a lay person and should provide opportunity for each participant to be involved.

What is the purpose of the new members class?

There are actually five "purposes." They include:

1) *Orientation* in which the history, tradition, and purpose of the congregation is explored.
2) *Evangelism* in which the meaning and challenge of commitment to Christ is explored.
3) *Teaching* in which the faith of the church is explored, and the worship and sacraments of the church are explained.
4) *Relationships* in which the bonds of friendship are developed.
5) *Challenge* in which opportunities for involvement and service are explored.

One final observation about the purpose of the new members class. While all of the above goals are valid, in the judgment of several authorities, the *primary* purpose of the class should be relational.

Tasks for Incorporation

The following tasks should be identified as responsibilities of the local church in meeting its responsibilities in the member incorporation process:

1. Identify and respond to needs;
2. Communicate clearly the identity of the congregation;
3. Encourage concern for the well-being of the congregation;
4. Help people in the joining process;
5. Prepare people for belonging;
6. Provide a meaningful reception.

Let's look at each task...

1. Identify and respond to needs.

When people unite with a congregation, they have hopes and expectations which they anticipate will be met in this community of believers. They also come with a history, including images of and experiences with the church. It is important to provide an opportunity for people to tell their story. It will be helpful for people to recall and relate specific elements of their history, including their experiences with the church. People also may be encouraged to relate something of their spiritual journey and their expectations as they make a new commitment. To encourage this enables people to feel they are known, and that they belong. It also helps minimize the possibility of false expectations, and so reduces the danger of new members becoming dropouts.

Oswald and Leas[4] point out that encouraging newcomers to talk about the things they valued in a past congregation will help clarify expectations for membership in this church. They also suggest the value of affording newcomers the opportunity to deal with any unresolved grief about leaving their former parish. If one's heart and soul are in the previous parish, it will be difficult to fit in and feel part of a new church family.

It is not uncommon to find that among those joining the church are some people who have been hurt or disappointed by a congregation in the past. Sometimes the pain is the result of a church's failure or insensitivity toward the person while a member; other times it results from a feeling of betrayal because of a sin or failure in the leaders of the former congregation; still other instances may be the result of conflict with someone in the previous parish. In any event, new associations cannot truly develop until old ones are healed, and so as people explore affiliation they must be helped to recognize and deal with the pain of the past.

Opportunity also ought to be provided for a discussion of expectations. New members will have the hope that life in this congregation will mean help in dealing with important issues; guidance and strength for one's spiritual journey; support in a time of need. If the church is clear about its role and functions, and sets forth what people have a right to expect from it, a process is established which enables a comparison of what a prospective member may anticipate and what the congregation is committed to provide.

This area of concern can be dealt with most effectively in a small group discussion. If your new members class is set up to provide for that, the first two or three small group sessions can deal with these issues. The small group lay leader will have been provided with material and questions to get people started talking, and lively discussion will

follow.   During the discussion times needs and
concerns will be identified by the lay leader, who
will be able to plan appropriate ways to deal with
these issues in future class sessions.

2. *Clearly communicate the church's identity.*

If people are to "belong" they need to know
and identify with the history, tradition, philosophy
and goals of the congregation. As people move into
membership they need to be acquainted with this
information. One needs to know and accept what
the church is before a valid decision can be made
about participation in and identification with that
body. A congregation will want to communicate
clearly its identity, and will have planned a method
by which newcomers are enabled to understand the
uniqueness of this particular part of the family of
God.

One good way to meet this need is to invite a
long-time member of the church to come in and tell
the story of the church, and that member's own
story of   involvement.   Anniversary booklets,
pictures, and other historical items may be used.
This personalized history is designed to help
newcomers understand, and enter into, the story of
the church, so that it becomes their story as well.

It will also be helpful to distribute the
church directory, brochure and any other materials
which are helpful in acquainting newcomers with
the life and ministry of the church.

3. *Encourage a concern for the well-being of the congregation.*

New members of a congregation will be
interested in what they can give to the church, as
well as in what they will receive. While it is true

that it is more blessed to give than to receive, it is equally true that one cannot give without having first received. We have dealt with receiving first, therefore, but do not wish to suggest that it is the primary concern of newcomers. Many of those joining the church come out of a fresh experience of grace. They are eager to learn ways in which they may express gratitude to God and contribute to the well-being of the congregation.

On one occasion in my ministry a man in late middle age joined our congregation. His involvement with church had been very limited, but he joined with enthusiasm and began attending faithfully. One day he came to me and said he would like to serve the church in some way as an expression of his gratitude. After thinking about his offer I gave his name to our usher's committee and soon he was involved in that activity. After a Sunday service, he approached me again and said, "I am happy to take my turn at ushering, but I was looking for something to do that would make a difference." I have not forgotten that lesson. Most new members want to make a meaningful contribution to a worthwhile purpose.

What provision does your congregation make to encourage concern for ministry? The pattern in many congregations is to try and find a person to fill every job, when what we ought to do is find some job for every person in the church. Not just any job, but one which provides an opportunity for a person to make a meaningful contribution.

In order to accomplish that, a congregation should develop a method to help incoming members identify their interests in and gifts for ministry, and to explore opportunities for service in and through the congregation. Many congregations provide for this process in the new members class.

Often, forms are prepared which provide both for gift identification and ministry opportunities.[5] It may be that people find and begin their service even before membership officially begins.

Dealing with concern for the well-being of the congregation involves clarifying expectations for members of the church. One of my earliest pastoral memories is of making a call on a family who had joined the church several years before, but in the memory of the church leaders had not attended since. In the course of a visit with them, the man made this statement: "Nobody told me that if I joined I was expected to attend." That may be an extreme case, but it raises a real issue. Do those who join your congregation know what is expected of them?

Stewardship responsibility ought also to be dealt with prior to membership. Prospective members have a right to know the congregation's budget, the approach to financial needs, and the general expectations about giving. Biblical principles of stewardship can be communicated. If the congregation has expectations in other areas of the Christian life, they should be openly discussed. No one is helped when expectations are discovered as surprises after a person has become a member.

4. Help people in the joining process.

This includes providing a specific publicized method of introducing people to membership and orienting them to the congregation. As has been discussed, that calls for some kind of pre-membership class. By promoting the class the congregation is already helping people in the joining process. This class will deal with the process and methods by which people join, as well as the content of the meetings and/or services in which joining takes place.

In many traditions not all new members join the congregation in the same way. A review of methods of joining will help participants explore the various options. If a person is joining from membership in another congregation, will a certificate of transfer be required? If so, what is the process of securing it? Is other information required? All questions about the process of becoming a member should be reviewed in the membership class.

In the congregation I most recently served, we always discussed two events. The first was the meeting with the congregation's spiritual leaders (the board of elders), where actual enrollment in membership took place. It is essential that class participants know what to expect at such a time since they may be somewhat apprehensive. The more information which can be provided in advance, the lower the level of anxiety. Not only should the format of the meeting be discussed, but questions which will be asked of class members should be carefully explained so participants understand their significance and know how to reply.

The second occasion calling for review is the worship service at which new members will be received. Once again, care should be taken to insure that participants understand what is expected of them, how the service will be conducted, and what is asked of the new members. Especially important is the understanding of promises being made.

Congregations effective in helping visitors become members give careful attention to helping people in the joining process.

5. Prepare people for belonging.

Joining and belonging are separate issues. While all members of the congregation know that they have joined, not all feel that they belong. Studies have suggested that as many as one third of the members of a congregation may feel that they do not truly belong.[6]

In one sense it is true to say that belonging comes before joining. The feelings of acceptance and inclusion produce the decision to join. In another sense, belonging is an ongoing need which is enhanced by what happens before, during and after the joining process. The feeling of belonging is the result of being part of a community of people who know us, accept us, and care about us. When we belong, loneliness is vanquished, hope and strength renewed, and new beginnings made possible.

"When belonging happens, joining takes on new meaning — much more than a ritual performed in a hurried moment at the end of a worship service. The joining becomes a celebration of the belonging already extended by the congregation and experienced by the new member. It is an outward and visible sign of the bonding that has already occurred. The membership ritual proclaims to all that the people belong to one another in Christ, as members of a community of faith and fellowship. It affirms that 'you belong to us, and we belong to one another'."[7]

6. Provide a meaningful experience of reception.

The goal is to enable those being received into membership to feel that this is a wonderfully memorable occasion. Membership is made meaningful in part by a public service of reception which makes a deep and lasting impression on those who are uniting with the church. It has been pointed out that in the early centuries of the church's life, the act of joining the church was a powerful and dramatic event. At one point in the process prospective members, in the presence of the congregation, stood before a book called "The Book of Life." One by one they made their vows of membership, and then wrote their name in the book. One would not easily forget such an experience.

The method by which new memoers are received varies with the tradition of the congregation. Whatever the tradition, the reception of members should be carefully planned and never appear rushed. For that reason it ought not be placed at the end of the worship service. A few suggestions about the service of reception may add meaning for those being received. Those being received into membership should be seated at the front of the sanctuary, and be ushered to their places as the service begins, escorted by one or more members of the congregation. If the congregation uses new member sponsors to assist in the incorporation process, they may accompany the new member with whom they have been united.

During the service of reception, the new members are introduced individually by the pastor, who stands with them facing the congregation. In some churches the pastor conducts a brief interview with each person being received. If that is to be done, the new member will have been informed of questions which will be asked. Suzanne Braden suggests that the pastor "share with the congregation one of the reasons the person is joining, with a statement like: 'John is joining us partly because he wants to participate in our ministry with street people', or 'Denise says that our sanctuary and worship service help her feel close to God'."[8]

Since the service of reception is an expression of commitment to God, the spiritual aspects are the major focus. In some churches the pastor selects a Scripture verse appropriate for each new member, reads it from a card on which it has been printed, and then hands it to the new member. Individual prayer, perhaps accompanied by the laying on of hands, is also appropriate. The moment of making vows is treated with seriousness and reverence.

At some point the members of the congregation may be asked to stand and make a promise to receive and support these new members as part of the body. Perhaps they will be asked to reaffirm their own commitment to Christ and his body. In some churches new members sign the congregation's membership book at this point in the service.

After the formal actions of reception are completed, a personal and individual welcome may be given to each new member, by the pastor and/or by a lay member who welcomes on behalf of the congregation. Often a membership certificate or a Bible is given to mark the occasion. When the service is concluding, new members may be escorted to the rear of the worship area where they will be welcomed by departing worshippers.

In congregations where newcomers are generally received into membership on three or four "special Sundays" throughout the year, the entire service may be planned around this event. Invitations might be prepared and sent to the family and friends of those being received.

It may be possible to have pictures taken of the new members prior to the worship service. If a bulletin board has been prepared in advance, pictures of new members can be prominently displayed immediately after their reception. Later, those pictures can be used in a newsletter article about the newcomers. Let the pictures remain displayed until the next new members are received. Perhaps the pictures will be displayed again later, either with those of others who joined during the year, or at their first anniversary of membership. The purpose of all this is to help new members feel that they have not only joined, but belong.

The Fifth Goal in Evangelization

We have suggested that evangelization is a process, and that it is not complete until those who have responded to Jesus Christ, and become actively involved in a local congregation, are living out a life of discipleship. The ministry of the church involves calling people to, and equipping them for, life in God's kingdom. That ministry is the on-going task of the church, and is addressed to all of those who have become, and are becoming, followers of Christ. Brief mention is made here of three crucial ingredients in the life of discipleship which will be lifted up as norms for the life of a citizen of the kingdom.

1. *A life of personal obedience.* Obedience to Christ is a basic ingredient in the New Testament's depiction of the Christian life. The church needs to be faithful in declaring that. We are to proclaim Jesus Christ not only as Savior, but as Lord. Much harm has been caused by the failure to be clear about the cost of discipleship. We do no one a favor

by offering cheap grace. Christians are called to obedience.

2. *A life of winsome witness.* Witness is a basic ingredient in the New Testament's depiction of the Christian life. Every follower of Jesus is called to share Christ's love and make known his salvation. Our task is to relate to people in love, to deal with all persons respectfully and graciously, to do what we can to encourage them, and to be ready to offer our witness. We will want to "always be prepared to give an answer to everyone who asks you to give the reason for the hope that you have. But do this with gentleness and respect..." (I Peter 3:15, 16 NIV). Every Christian is called to participate in the task of evangelism.

3. *A life of active service.* Service is a basic ingredient in the New Testament's depiction of the Christian life. The example and the call of Christ clearly reveal the importance of ministering to human need. Our Lord pointed out that the signs of his kingdom include the hungry being fed, the sick ministered to, prisoners visited, water shared. Our responsibility is to use the means and opportunities given us, where we are, to minister to human need. Christians are called to a life of service in the world.

      All this is part of the ministry of an evangelizing congregation, whose love and concern for people continues, as Paul put it, "until we all attain to the unity of the faith and of the knowledge of the Son of God, to mature adulthood, to the measure of the stature of the fullness of Christ ... speaking the truth in love, we are to grow up in every way into him who is the head, into Christ, from whom the whole body, joined and knit together by every joint with which it is supplied, when each part is working properly, makes bodily growth and upbuilds itself in love." (Eph. 4:13-16).

Our journey together has nearly reached its end. We have spoken about many ways by which you and your congregation can help people to come to faith; to believe and belong — both to God and to the family of God. That task requires intentional effort. It calls for a commitment and a plan. But the task is also joyful and rewarding. Seeing people become alive in Christ and actively involved in the life and ministry of the congregation is a source of joy for newcomer and congregation alike. It is also what Christ calls us to be about.

---

1 *The First Year*, p. vi.
2 The most helpful treatment of the process, in my judgment, is by Lyle Schaller, *Assimilating New Members*, (Nashville, Abingdon Press, 1978).
3 The Win Arn Growth Report, "Making Your New Members Class Work." No. 4
4 *The Inviting Church*, p. 61.
5 A sample of such a form is included in Appendix B.
6 Braden, *op cit*, p. 10.
7 Donald F. LaSuer and L. Ray Sells, *Bonds of Belonging*, (Nashville: Discipleship Resources), p. 17.
8 *The First Year*, p. 51.

Reflection Questions — Chapter Eight

1. What is your congregation's strategy and practice regarding new members classes?

2. How many new members classes did you offer in the past year? How many are planned for this year? Next year?

3. What do you believe is the primary purpose of the new members class?

4. What do you believe to be the key tasks in incorporation? Which do you feel needs attention most urgently?

5. What helps a person belong?

6. How does your congregation help people understand expectations for members?

7. What is distinctive in the identity of your congregation?

8. Think back to your last service for the reception of new members. How could it be made more effective?

9. What procedure do you follow to enable new members to discover a gift for ministry? How do you help them find a task or role in ministry?

10. In reviewing the characteristics of incorporated members, which qualities are specifically dealt with in your new members class? Which are overlooked?

11. In what ways does your congregation deal with the fifth goal in evangelization?

12. What three words best describe your view of evangelism?

Postlude

The church is called by its Lord to be in mission. Evangelism is one part of that mission. We are called to reach out to — and receive — those for whom the church is in mission. That is a critical part of evangelism. The great work of evangelism could be approached and discussed in many different ways. One way has been developed in this book. It is a way that has been called "church growth."

Some people dislike the term, believing that it sounds self-serving. That danger does exist, and we must be on guard against seeking new members for our sake. When we are guilty of that, we must repent. Evangelism cannot be cheapened into meaning nothing more than recruitment. And recruitment which has as its goal the advancement of the church as institution deserves severe criticism.

However, if we believe that the church is one of God's great gifts, that it is the body of Christ on earth, and that our congregation is a wonderful manifestation of Christ's body, we will rightfully want to share it. And if our purpose in reaching out to people and encouraging their entrance into and involvement in the life of the church is that they too may enjoy God's gift, such reaching out is holy and right. And if we have found fellowship with God in our church, and find it there still, and are helped by our church to grow in our love and service to God, we would be wrong not to invite others to share with us in the life of our congregation.

It is in such conviction that this book has been written, and in that hope that it is sent forth.

Appendix A

New Member Survey

When this survey is sent out, it should be accompanied by a letter of explanation. That letter will indicate why the survey is being taken, and what will be done with the results. It is wise to inform people that results will be tabulated and sent to those who participate in the survey, and that they will be kept informed about what develops from those results. Tabulated survey results should be sent out as promptly as possible.

You may want to survey all those who have become members of your church within the past two years. If you have received a large number of new members within the past year (50 or more) the survey may well focus on just that group.

New Member Survey

Your Name _____

Month and year you joined this church _____

(Suggested Questions)

1. The first time you attended our church, what brought you?
2. What led you to make a return visit?
3. Who did the most to make you feel welcome here?
4. How long did you attend here before you decided to join?
5. What made you want to join?
6. What made you hesitate?
7. Just prior to coming here, had you been an active member of any other church?
8. How did you first become aware of this church?
9. How would you describe your experience of the new member orientation process?
10. In which groups or activities of the church are you currently participating?
11. Is there a group or activity in which you might wish to participate?
12. What role or task do you have in our church?
13. If you were to invite a friend to worship, how do you think your friend would perceive the visit?
14. What are your feelings about our worship services?
15. Do you have any concerns about our church you wish to share?
16. Now that you are a member, how well has our church fulfilled your expectations?

Appendix B

Ministry Opportunities

This sample form is designed to help your new members identify areas of ministry in which they can serve, and to become aware of, and select, appropriate tasks or roles which they can fulfill. It will, of course, contain the opportunities offered for service through the ministries of your church.

Two possible ways for introducing the form are suggested:

a) It is presented in the new members class, after appropriate explanation and discussion.
b) It is presented as part of a class taught on spiritual gifts.

The ideal is to have each member of the church complete the form, and the completed forms become the source from which new workers are selected.

MINISTRY OPPORTUNITIES

Name _____

Address _____

Phone _____ Business Phone _____

Occupation _____

Birth date _____

	Previous Experience	Now Doing	Interested in

Children's Ministry

	Previous Experience	Now Doing	Interested in
a. Teaching Church School	____	____	____
b. Vacation Bible School	____	____	____
c. Nursery	____	____	____
d. Children's Church	____	____	____
e. Youth Club	____	____	____
f. Children's Ministry Comm.	____	____	____
g. Library	____	____	____

Youth Ministry

	Previous Experience	Now Doing	Interested in
a. Teaching Church School	____	____	____
b. Sponsor Group Fellowship	____	____	____
c. Senior High Fellowship	____	____	____
d. Small Group Leader	____	____	____
e. Camp Counselor	____	____	____
f. Boy Scouts	____	____	____
g. College			
- Teaching a class	____	____	____
- Sponsor Group Fellowship	____	____	____
- Foreign Students	____	____	____

Adult Ministry

	Previous Experience	Now Doing	Interested in
a. Teaching Church School	____	____	____
b. Stephen Ministry	____	____	____
c. Bethel Bible Series			
- Congregational	____	____	____
- In Depth	____	____	____
d. Small Groups			
- Lead	____	____	____
- Participate	____	____	____
e. Helping with Weddings	____	____	____

f. Special Topics for Classes
   (specify)   _____   _____   _____
g. Library   _____   _____   _____
h. Prayer Chain   _____   _____   _____
i. Adult Ministry Committee   _____   _____   _____

Service   Ministry

a. Ministry to Senior Citizens
   - Visitation   _____   _____   _____
   - Transportation   _____   _____   _____
   - Adopt a Shut-In   _____   _____   _____
   - Outreach to Aging   _____   _____   _____
b. Ministry to Sick
   - Home Visitation   _____   _____   _____
   - Nursing Home Visits   _____   _____   _____
   - Providing short term care   _____   _____   _____
c. Ushers   _____   _____   _____
d. Carpentry & Maintenance   _____   _____   _____
e. Special Short Term Needs
   - Housing   _____   _____   _____
   - Food   _____   _____   _____
   - Baby Sitting   _____   _____   _____
   - Provide Transportation   _____   _____   _____
f. Prison Ministry
   - Visitation   _____   _____   _____
   - Bible Study Leader   _____   _____   _____
g. Study and Advocacy
   - Local issues   _____   _____   _____
   - National issues   _____   _____   _____
   - International issues   _____   _____   _____

Evangelism

a. Visitation   _____   _____   _____
b. Phone   _____   _____   _____
c. Evangelistic Bible Study   _____   _____   _____
d. Committee   _____   _____   _____

Mission

a. Foreign Emphasis   _____   _____   _____
b. Local Emphasis   _____   _____   _____
c. Church Mission Projects   _____   _____   _____
d. Committee   _____   _____   _____

Worship

a. Music
   - Choir Member   _____   _____   _____
   - Vocal Music   _____   _____   _____
   - Accompanist   _____   _____   _____
   - Instrument   _____   _____   _____
   - Bell Choir   _____   _____   _____
   - Youth Choir Ass't.   _____   _____   _____
   - Song Leader   _____   _____   _____
   - Child/Youth Choirs Ass't. _____   _____   _____
   - Asst. Adult Choir Director _____   _____   _____
b. Drama   _____   _____   _____
c. Worship Services
   - Lay Leader   _____   _____   _____
   - Planning Committee   _____   _____   _____
   - Usher   _____   _____   _____
   - Floral Arrangements   _____   _____   _____
d. Dance   _____   _____   _____
e. Sound/Recording Equipment _____   _____   _____
f. Provide Transportation   _____   _____   _____

Women's Ministries

a. Bible Study Leader   _____   _____   _____
b. Participate in Small Group _____   _____   _____
c. Provide Child Care   _____   _____   _____

Food Pantry

a. Provide Food/Clothing   _____   _____   _____
b. Work in Pantry   _____   _____   _____

Fellowship   Committee

a. Greet at Worship Services   _____   _____   _____
b. Serve as Host/Hostess   _____   _____   _____
c. Entertain Guests of the church
    in my home   _____   _____   _____

Publicity and Visual Arts

a. Writing   _____   _____   _____
b. Crafts   _____   _____   _____
c. Photography   _____   _____   _____
d. Audio—Visual   _____   _____   _____
e. Banners   _____   _____   _____
f. Work on Newsletter   _____   _____   _____

Financial/Accounting   _____   _____   _____

Clerical

a. Typing   _____   _____   _____
b. Phoning   _____   _____   _____
c. Addressing Envelopes   _____   _____   _____
d. Other   _____   _____   _____

Lay Ministry

a. Counseling   _____   _____   _____
b. Vocational Guidance   _____   _____   _____
c. Financial Planning   _____   _____   _____
d. Refugee Resettlement   _____   _____   _____
e. Tutoring   _____   _____   _____
f. Other   _____   _____   _____

YOUR INTEREST PRIORITY

Of the areas of service in which you are interested, please show where you would most like to serve:

1. _____

2. _____

3. _____

Special skills I would be willing to share:

_____

_____

Professional or educational background useful in services through the church:

_____

Are you currently involved in any community ministry or service?

If so, please explain: _____

_____

_____

Appendix C

Task Force Work Sheet

This form is provided to assist the task force in carrying out its function, and to monitor progress as it works to fulfill its responsibilities. The task force leader is responsible for keeping the work sheet updated, and reviewing it regularly with the group. Since the format it follows will depend on the plans and goals the group will set, it cannot be outlined in full until the task force has done a good part of its work. The form does provide specific data for the initial work of the task force. The group is encouraged to follow the same plan until its work is complete.

NEED	STEPS TO TAKE
1. Community Analysis	a. Ministry Area Defined
	b. Target Group Selected
	c. Ministry Needs Identified
2. Congregational Preparation	a. Vision Communicated
	b. Regular Prayer for Outreach Occurring
	c. Qualities of Congregational life addressed
	d. Mission Statement Reviewed
3. Congregational Analysis	a. Membership Statistics Reviewed
	b. Age-Range Study Completed
	c. Average Worship Attendance Reviewed
	d. Congregational Strengths Identified
	e. Present Ministries and Workers Studied
4. Report to Governing Board	a. Preparation of a Plan
	b. Recommendation of Outreach Goals
	c. Suggested Strategies

PERSON RESPONSIBLE   DATE IMPLEMENTED
                                OR COMPLETED

_____   _____
_____   _____
_____   _____

_____   _____

_____   _____

_____   _____

_____   _____

_____   _____

_____   _____

_____   _____

_____   _____

_____   _____

_____   _____

_____   _____
_____   _____

Suggested Reading List

Armstrong, Richard Stoll. *Service Evangelism*. Philadelphia: The Westminster Press, 1979.

Arn, Win. *The Church Growth Ratio Book*. Pasadena: Church Growth, Inc., 1987.

————. *The Master's Plan for Making Disciples*. Pasadena: Church Growth, Inc., 1982.

————. Carroll Nyquist and Charles Arn. *Who Cares About Love?* Pasadena: Church Growth Press, 1986.

Baehr, Theodore. *Getting the Word Out*. New York: Harper and Row, 1986.

Baker, Wesley. *The Vital Signs*. A Good News Series. New York: The Program Agency of the United Presbyterian Church in the USA, 1978.

Braden, Suzanne. *The First Year*. Nashville: Discipleship Resources, 1987.

Callahan, Kennon L. *Twelve Keys to an Effective Church*. San Francisco: Harper and Row, Publishers, 1983.

Dunkin, Steve. *Church Advertising: A Practical Guide*. Nashville: Abingdon Press, 1982.

FOCUS, Concepts of Ministry and Goals for the Local Church. Grand Rapids: Christian Reformed Home Missions, 1987. Available from the Reformed Church in

America Distribution Center, 3000 Ivanrest, S.W.,
Grandville, MI 49418.

Gallup, George. *The Unchurched American, 1988.*
Princeton: The Gallup Organization, 1988.

Gribbon, R. T. *When People Seek the Church.*
Washington: The Alban Institute.

————. *Half the Congregation: Ministry with 18-40
Year Olds.* Washington: The Alban Institute.

Harre, Alan F. *Close the Back Door.* St. Louis:
Concordia Publishing House, 1984.

Heck, Joel D. *Make Disciples.* St. Louis: Concordia,
1984.

Hinson, William H. *A Place to Dig In.* Nashville:
Abingdon Press, 1987.

Hunter III, George G. *To Spread the Power.* Nashville:
Abingdon Press, 1987.

Johnson, Ben Campbell. *An Evangelism Primer.*
Atlanta: John Knox Press, 1983.

————. *Rethinking Evangelism.* Philadelphia: The
Westminster Press, 1987.

Johnson, Douglas W. *Reaching Out to the Unchurched.*
Valley Forge: Judson Press, 1983.

LaSuer, and L. Ray Sells. *Bonds of Belonging.*
Nashville: Discipleship Resources.

McIntosh, Duncan and Richard E. Rusbuldt. *Planning Growth in Your Church.* Valley Forge: Judson Press, 1983.

Miller, Herb. *Fishing on the Asphalt.* St. Louis: Bethany Press, 1983.

————. *Evangelism's Open Secrets.* St. Louis: C B P Press, 1984.

————. *How to Build A Magnetic Church.* Nashville: Abingdon Press, 1987.

Oswald, Roy M. and Speed B. Leas. *The Inviting Church.* Washington: The Alban Institute, 1987.

Reeves, R. Daniel and Ronald Jenson. *Always Advancing: Modern Strategies for Church Growth.* San Bernadino: Here's Life Publishers, Inc., 1984.

Research Report. "Congregational Tools for Effective Evangelism Project. The American Lutheran Church. October, 1986.

Routhauge, Arlin J. *Sizing Up A Congregation.* New York: The Episcopal Church Center.

Savage, John S. *The Apathetic and Bored Church Member.* Pittsford: Lead Consultants, 1976.

Schaller, Lyle. *Activating the Passive Church.* Nashville: Abingdon Press,1981.

————. *Assimilating New Members.* Creative Leadership Series. Nashville: Abingdon Press, 1978.

————. *Growing Plans.* Nashville: Abingdon Press, 1983.

————. *44 Ways to Increase Church Attendance.* Nashville: Abingdon Press, 1988.

————. "Where Are the Visitors?" CHURCH MANAGEMENT - THE CLERGY JOURNAL, April, 1984.

Wagner, C. Peter. *Strategies for Church Growth.* Ventura: Regal Books, Division of GL Publications, 1987.

Walrath, Douglas. *Frameworks: Patterns of Living and Believing Today.* Pilgrim Press, 1987.

Watson, David. *Discipleship.* London: Hodder and Stoughton, 1981.